Twayne's United States Authors Series

EDITOR OF THIS VOLUME

Warren French

Indiana University

Norman Mailer

TUSAS 322

NORMAN MAILER

By ROBERT MERRILL
University of Nevada

TWAYNE PUBLISHERS
A DIVISION OF G. K. HALL & CO., BOSTON

Copyright © 1978 by G. K. Hall & Co.

Published in 1978 by Twayne Publishers,
A Division of G. K. Hall & Co.
All Rights Reserved

Printed on permanent/durable acid-free paper and bound
in the United States of America

Frontispiece photo of Norman Mailer © by Jill Krementz

Library of Congress Cataloging in Publication Data

Merrill, Robert, 1944-
Norman Mailer.

(Twayne's United States authors series ; TUSAS 322)
Bibliography: p. 161-65
Includes index.
1. Mailer, Norman—Criticism and interpretation.
PS3525.A4152Z77   813'.5'4   78-18357

ISBN 0-8057-7254-5

For My Parents

Contents

About the Author

Robert Merrill did his undergraduate work at the University of Utah and received his bachelor's degree in 1966. He then began graduate study at the University of Chicago, where he received his M.A. degree in 1967 and his Ph.D. in 1971. His dissertation was an extended critical study of Norman Mailer. Since 1971 Dr. Merrill has taught at the University of Nevada, Reno, where he is currently an Associate Professor of English. He has published essays on Shakespeare, recent Shakespearean criticism, Henry James, Herman Melville, Ernest Hemingway, Thomas Pynchon, Kurt Vonnegut, Joseph Heller, and Mailer in such journals as *Modern Language Quarterly, Texas Studies in Literature and Language, American Literature, Studies in American Fiction, Critique, Centennial Review, Western Humanities Review, Illinois Quarterly*, and *Ariel*. His reviews of books on Mailer have appeared in *Modern Philology* and *Western Humanities Review*. He is currently engaged in a book-length study of modern narrative tragedy which will focus on Ernest Hemingway. A latecomer to family life, Dr. Merrill lives in Reno with his wife, Dotson, and four cats, Wigglesworth, Sinookas, Sam, and Bayard.

Preface

It has not been easy to avoid Norman Mailer these last fifteen years. Since 1965 he has published twenty books; written, directed, and starred in three movies; dramatized *The Deer Park* off-Broadway; appeared on every television talk-show this side of the Iron Curtain; run for mayor of New York City; taken up three entire issues of *Harper's* with his accounts of the 1967 March on the Pentagon, the 1968 political conventions, and Women's Liberation, respectively; received the ultimate acknowledgment of a *Playboy* interview; spent a few well publicized days in jail, and aroused discussion in magazines and journals so diverse as *Look* and *Partisan Review*. No less than ten books have been published on his life or works. Like Muhammad Ali, Mailer has become a household word.

Honors have come Mailer's way in these years: election to the National Institute of Arts and Letters (1967) and the American Academy of Arts and Sciences (1970); the 1969 Pulitzer Prize in general nonfiction and the 1969 National Book Award in arts and letters (both for *The Armies of the Night*). He is rumored to have been one of four writers considered for the 1969 Nobel Prize in Literature (the others: André Malraux, W. H. Auden, and Samuel Beckett, the winner). And there have been more material rewards: Mailer is supposed to have made at least $500,000 with *An American Dream* (1965) and $450,000 with *Of a Fire on the Moon* (1970); more recently he received a contract from Little, Brown for somewhere in the area of one million dollars.[1] Mailer's career has begun to take on the appearance of the same American success story which in so many of his own books he attacks.

Curiously, however, Mailer's work is still not generally admired. He has won awards, made money, and publicized himself with remarkable success. *The Armies of the Night* (1968) won many converts among his critics. Yet Mailer's friends and foes alike have tended to agree that his achievement has not been "artistic" in nature. Most writing on Mailer has concerned itself with the man, his ideas, or his relationship to his period (his "representativeness").

Mailer's critical reputation is therefore suspect, for only when a writer's work is respected for its artistic value does it begin to enjoy a critical status commensurate with its popular success or notoriety.

To illustrate Mailer's anomalous critical reputation, I would ask who is being described in the following passage? "[He] lacks discipline, intelligence, honesty and a sense of the novel. His rhythms are erratic, his sense of character is nil, and he is as pretentious as a rich whore, as sentimental as a lollypop. Yet I think he has a large talent. His literary energy is enormous, and he had enough of a wild eye to go along with his instincts and so become the first figure for a new generation."[2] It happens that "he" is Jack Kerouac, not Norman Mailer. (The critic is of course Mailer himself; your average literary critic doesn't often suggest that a writer is "as pretentious as a rich whore.") But anyone who has read the published commentary on Mailer's works must be excused if he thought the quotation concerned Mailer. After all, what Mailer says about Kerouac has often been said of him: that he lacks everything but "talent." Somehow, the argument goes, there is *something* in Mailer, some "power" which he has never really harnessed to an appropriate literary form. It is a pity, but Mailer's is the example of "a great gift squandered."[3]

Three crucial assumptions are at work in most discussions of Mailer: (1) that his ideas are more interesting than his art, or in fact dominate—and so deserve more attention than—his art; (2) that his personality is more interesting than anything he has written, especially given that he is so "representative" a figure; (3) that he has squandered his great gift in works which impress more in their parts than their totality, works which fail precisely because Mailer has been too little the conscious artist.

Surely Mailer's ideas have engaged more commentators than the books in which they are expressed. Mailer has been treated as "a literary sociologist," "a literary terrorist," even, in one of his phases, a "dotty messiah";[4] he has been treated as almost everything except a literary artist. Even his much admired first novel, *The Naked and the Dead* (1948), did not inspire its reviewers or subsequent critics to congratulate him on his artistic success. Instead there was much talk about Mailer's critique of American society in general and the American army in particular. Early criticism on Mailer almost always reflects the belief that his social and political ideas are more interesting than his individual works. Thus we get Edmund Fuller writing on Mailer's sexual notions, Frederick Hoffman and George Schrader on Mailer's advocacy of Hip, and, most impressively, Diana

Trilling on Mailer's moral development.[5] Trilling's essay is perhaps the most discouraging of these studies, for it is one thing for an unsympathetic critic like Fuller to have little respect for Mailer's art, quite another for a sympathetic reader like Trilling to concede that Mailer's role as writer has been "more messianic than creative," and that he really is an "anti-artist." More recent critics have avoided such extreme judgments but have continued to focus on what one of them has called Mailer's "intellectual career," rather than his pretensions as a literary artist.[6]

Critics have just as often been fascinated by Mailer's public image. Harvey Swados once deplored the fact that Mailer was cashing in on the current "cult of personality" in American letters, thus receiving more attention than he deserved.[7] There is another side to this coin, however. In receiving this *kind* of attention, Mailer's works have seldom been judged on their literary merits. It is Mailer the man who has interested the media. We have been exposed to Mailer interviews in publications as unlikely as *Mademoiselle*;[8] we have been informed of Mailer's domestic problems, his court trials, his testimony on behalf of another man's "pornographic" novel;[9] we have been provided lengthy accounts of how Mailer now lives in *Life*, *Look*, and *Esquire*.[10] Mailer the man is so much a part of our culture, it is hardly surprising that critics have been quick to emphasize the figure behind the books. In so doing, however, they have usually failed to illuminate appreciably the nature of Mailer's art.

Dissatisfaction with this art often lies masked behind detours critics take in discussing his philosophy and personality. Implicit in all the discussions cited above, for example, is the assumption that Mailer's books will not sustain detailed aesthetic consideration—their interest lying elsewhere. This assumption is to be expected of readers who don't really value Mailer's books, but it is disturbing to find such sympathetic critics as Richard Foster arguing that Mailer, for all his virtues, "is not the finished and fully responsible writer-as-*artist* that many of his peers are."[11] This is a curious argument from someone who sees Mailer as our most impressive contemporary novelist. Finally it is not sufficient to praise Mailer, as Foster does, for "the obstinate vigor of [his] restless creativity," for "his ambitious fluency of expression," for "his ideas and his humanity"[12]—as if these qualities were divorced from the qualities of art! One must praise Mailer—wherever he deserves it—for exhibiting these qualities in realized works of art. The corollary, of course, is that one must also point out those occasions where Mailer fails to achieve anything like these effects. Only by making these aesthetic distinctions will we ever arrive at a just assessment of Mailer's importance as a writer.

It should be clear that my intention is to make just such an assessment. I have focused on questions of literary structure rather than "theme" and have avoided biographical speculation almost entirely. The thematic approach has been applied by many other critics, only occasionally with any success; the biographical approach threads its way through most discussions of Mailer, illuminating many things but seldom the work under consideration. It is remarkable that amidst the small library of critical materials on Mailer there nowhere exists the full-length aesthetic evaluation which usually precedes the study of a writer's intellectual or biographical dimensions. My book is intended to fill this gap.

In the chapters which follow I have been largely concerned with the aesthetic structure of Mailer's individual works, both his novels and works of nonfiction. Necessarily, then, I have often focused on the question of a work's unity or coherence. I am aware that unity and coherence are not synonymous with "success" or "greatness." Indeed, literary structure can be seen as irrelevant to a writer's success or failure, as Richard Poirier seems to suggest in his book *The Performing Self*: ". . . the literary structures which critics are so happy to locate are not so much equivalent to performance as merely the stage upon which it can take place. For a writer of great energy, structure may even be the element against which he is performing." Poirier argues that literary criticism has placed far too much emphasis on structure and thus on the "work," "the book or poem" as opposed to "writing as an act," or "performance." It happens that Mailer is one of his favorite examples of a contemporary "performer," one whose "writing" is much more interesting than whatever can be made of his "works."[13] It also happens that Poirier is one of Mailer's most perceptive and sympathetic critics. Therefore it is a bit embarrassing to suggest that if coherence doesn't *equate* with success, neither is structure the mechanical "stage" invoked in Poirier's discussion. Anyone who admires Mailer does so in part (usually in large part) because his works do exhibit the local energy and stylistic resources Poirier is always pointing to. But these local successes are not mere isolated beauties in a general ruin; the foundations of Mailer's works are solid enough, much sturdier than even Mailer's friendlier critics have acknowledged. I have assumed that the best answer to those who chide Mailer for his structural incoherences is not that such things don't matter, but that they don't exist (not, at least, in Mailer's better works).

My assumption is that the successful design of Mailer's better works gives point to and oversees those local instances of stylistic "energy" which in fact contribute to the design. In any case, I have said little about style and much about structure because it is structure which has been underacknowledged in Mailer's books. Poirier to the contrary, I don't see how Mailer can ever achieve the reputation he deserves if this acknowledgment is not forthcoming. For that matter, we will continue to have a very imperfect understanding of Mailer's failures unless we begin to focus our attention on the literary design of his individual works. For better or worse, Mailer's books succeed or fail in terms of their aesthetic form. The chapters which follow explore his successes and failures alike in just these terms.

Because I refer to three of Mailer's books repeatedly, I have cited them in the text with the following abbreviations: *Advertisements for Myself* as *Adv; The Presidential Papers* (New York: G. P. Putnam's Sons, 1963) as *TPP; Cannibals and Christians* (New York: Dial Press, 1966) as *CC*.

ROBERT MERRILL

University of Nevada, Reno

Acknowledgments

I want to thank the editors of the following journals for allowing me to use materials which first appeared in their pages: *Western Humanities Review, Illinois Quarterly, Centennial Review,* and *Aegis.*

I would also like to thank the following people who read portions of this book and made useful suggestions: Robert Streeter, James E. Miller, Jr., Robert Harvey, Richard Brown, Bernard Schopen, and most especially my wife, Dotson. My debt to Warren French, my editor, is very great. I would also thank Sheldon Sacks, whose excellent influence is imperfectly embodied in this book.

Chronology

1975 *The Fight.*
1976 *Genius and Lust: A Journey Through the Major Writings of Henry Miller.*

CHAPTER 1

Mailer as Man and Legend

IT may seem somewhat paradoxical to begin a study of Norman Mailer's artistic achievement by devoting a chapter—however brief—to Mailer's biography. There are several good reasons for doing so, however. The beginning student of Mailer's works deserves to know the basic facts underlying what Mailer himself refers to as his "legend."[1] Moreover, both beginning and advanced students should confront the problem of how difficult it is to apply the known facts of Mailer's life to the interpretation of his books. And even a brief review of Mailer's life will necessarily include an overview of his writing career, thus preparing for the critical discussions which will follow.

I   The Early Years: 1923–1959

Our major source of information on Mailer's life is of course Mailer himself. Since 1959 no less than fourteen of his books have described one or more of his personal experiences, and this does not count any of the so-called "autobiographical" novels. It is rather striking, then, that we still know next to nothing about the first twenty years of Mailer's life. Mailer almost never alludes to his childhood, and even his fictional heroes are notoriously reticent about their "formative" years. Why this should be so is something of a mystery, but Mailer offers a strong hint towards an answer in *The Armies of the Night*. At one point he writes of his emotions while watching a group of young men turn in their draft cards to protest the war in Vietnam:

. . . as they did this, a deep gloom began to work on Mailer, because a deep modesty was on its way to him, he could feel himself becoming more and more of a modest man as he stood there in the cold with his hangover, and he hated this because modesty was an old family relative, he had been born to a modest family, had been a modest boy, a modest young man, and he hated that, he loved the pride and the arrogance and the confidence and the

17

egocentricity he had acquired over the years, that was his force and his luxury and the iron in his greed, the richest sugar of his pleasure, the strength of his competitive force . . .[2]

Mailer's "modest" boyhood is clearly something he would rather forget. The rejection of his Jewish heritage is probably crucial here, for Mailer has said that he grew up in "the most secure Jewish environment in America"[3] and that the one self-image he finds intolerable is that of a nice Jewish boy from Brooklyn. At the present time, however, such theories must remain speculation.

What we do know about Mailer's early years tends to suggest that he was a model son, what we would call an "achiever." Born in 1923 to Isaac and Fanny Mailer, Mailer grew up in Brooklyn and graduated from Boys High School in 1939. An excellent student, he entered Harvard at the age of sixteen and earned a B.S. degree in aeronautical engineering in 1943. While at Harvard he began to write fiction, winning several short story contests and completing two unpublished novels before entering the army in 1944. That same year he married Beatrice Silverman, the first of his four wives.

Mailer served in the Pacific Ocean at Leyte and Luzon before returning home in 1946 to begin writing *The Naked and the Dead*. The publication of this novel in 1948 was almost surely the turning point in Mailer's life. Like Melville, Mailer has pointed to his twenty-fifth year as the beginning of his "real" existence, for with the enormous success of *The Naked and the Dead* his life was altered irrevocably:

My farewell to an average man's experience was too abrupt; never again would I know, in the dreary way one usually knows such things, what it was like to work at a dull job, or take orders from a man one hated. If I had had a career of that in the army, it now was done—there was nothing left in the first twenty-four years of my life to write about; one way or another, my life seeemed to have been mined and melted into the long reaches of the book. And so I was prominent and empty, and I had to begin life again . . . (*Adv*, 92).

There can be little question that in 1948 Mailer did begin to refashion his life and therefore his personality. The young man who wrote *The Naked and the Dead* was still modest enough to tell an interviewer, "I think it's much better when people who read your book don't know anything about you, even what you look like."[4] Eleven years later, this man had transformed to an extent where he could confess that his major desire was to make "a revolution in the consciousness of our time" (*Adv*, 17). Obviously something remarkable had occurred in Mailer's life between 1948 and 1959.

It is easier to remark upon this change than to specify what brought it about. Mailer has discussed this period of his life at great length in *Advertisements for Myself* (1959), so we might assume that a careful reading of this work would provide ample biographical evidence. In point of fact, however, the information offered in *Advertisements* is highly selective. Here we discover that Mailer worked as a scriptwriter in Hollywood during 1949-1950; that he and his first wife were divorced in 1952; that he married Adele Morales in 1954; that he lived in Mexico at different times in the early 1950s; that he cofounded *The Village Voice* in 1955 and subsequently became a columnist for that Greenwich Village newspaper; that he experimented with sex and drugs, especially while he was writing his third novel, *The Deer Park*. Beyond these bare facts, however, Mailer tells us surprisingly little about his personal life.

Of course, *Advertisements* also reminds us that it was during this period that Mailer wrote two rather unpopular novels, *Barbary Shore* (1951) and *The Deer Park* (1955); a number of short stories (collected in *Advertisements*); and one of the more important essays of the postwar period, "The White Negro" (1957). Ultimately, these are the crucial "facts" of the period in question, not only for those of us who admire Mailer's art but for Mailer himself. Mailer introduces biographical materials only when they are relevant to the growth of his ideas and/or individual works, and even then it isn't always clear whether he means to argue for a direct relationship between his life and his art. Two examples should suggest the tenuous connection between what we know of Mailer's life and his published works.

One of the more revealing sections of *Advertisements* concerns the composition, publication, and critical reception of *The Deer Park* (*Adv*, 228–64). In the course of this lengthy essay, Mailer discloses much of what we know about his experiences in Mexico, his experiments with marijuana and peyote, and his quarrels with various New York publishers. The subject matter and tone of this piece almost seem "confessional." But what does the essay really tell us about the nature of Mailer's third novel? In an interview with Mailer, I once asked him to comment on my theory that *The Deer Park* was his most autobiographical novel. (I had in mind the relationship between Charley Eitel and Elena Esposito, which I took to be a fictional reworking of Mailer's second marriage.) Mailer acknowledged the "personal" sources of the book but declined to elaborate.[5] His essay on *The Deer Park* is even more reticent on this subject. This points up the fact that Mailer's personal "revelations," here and elsewhere, are seldom introduced to "explain" his works. In his personal essays, Mailer contributes odd pieces of lore concerning his life, but these details neither constitute a "thoroughgoing autobiography" (*Adv*, 107) nor assist materially in the interpretation of his art.

The genesis of Mailer's most famous essay, "The White Negro," is an even more telling example. First published in 1957 and reprinted in *Advertisements*, "The White Negro" analyzes the postwar phenomenon of the hipster, that violent American rebel whom Mailer defends in his most impassioned rhetoric. It might be argued that the whole of *Advertisements* is intended to explain Mailer's conversion to this "cause." Early sections of the book describe his youthful commitment to political liberalism, then revolutionary socialism; later sections trace his rejection of rationality as an adequate guide to life's complexities. Gradually, over a period of almost ten years, Mailer discarded his liberal and socialistic sympathies and turned to what he called an "American existentialism," roughly embodied in the hipster and characterized by a deep commitment to instinct as opposed to reason. "The White Negro" climaxed one of the most startling intellectual reversals in American literary history.[6]

Mailer's philosophical shift during this period was therefore drastic, but what led to this change? His war experiences wouldn't seem to be the answer, for Mailer's serious commitment to socialism dates from 1948 to 1951. His stay in Hollywood may have been crucial, but he has never offered a detailed account of that period. The experiments with sex, alcohol, and drugs were obviously relevant, but Mailer's many references to these experiences hardly constitute more than random hints. Finally, Mailer's second marriage may well have been decisive; but he has revealed virtually nothing about this marriage. The plain truth is that we don't know what prompted Mailer's intellectual about-face. We don't even know if his personal experiences were more important than his reading during this period, for the latter has never really been examined.

We do know that *Advertisements for Myself* was as decisive for Mailer's career as *The Naked and the Dead* had been for his personal life. Written in the wake of Mailer's popular and critical failures with

Barbary Shore and *The Deer Park, Advertisements* reveals the emergence of that proud, arrogant, and egocentric personality Mailer celebrates in *The Armies of the Night.* The emergence of Mailer's "legend" dates from this year, too, though Mailer has been filling in its contours for the last twenty years. After the publication of *Advertisements,* it would be a long time before anyone would accuse Mailer of being a nice Jewish boy from Brooklyn.

II *The Later Years: 1959–1978*

Mailer's tone throughout *Advertisements* is calculated to offend most of his readers, but the source of his first real notoriety was "The White Negro," specifically the passage in which he defends as "courageous" the murder of a candy store keeper by "two strong eighteen-year-old hoodlums" (*Adv,* 347). While this defense is heavily qualified and extends the essay's total argument, it is hardly surprising that the American public was less than charmed by such "logic" as embodied in the following: "The psychopath murders—if he has the courage—out of the necessity to purge his violence, for if he cannot empty his hatred then he cannot love, his being is frozen with implacable self-hatred for his cowardice" (*Adv,* 347). But of course few men achieve legendary status because of what they *write.* What insured Mailer's dubious reputation was the single most unfortunate event of his life: the stabbing of his second wife less than a year after the publication of *Advertisements.*

Mailer stabbed his wife with a penknife on November 19, 1960, in the aftermath of a rather bizarre party celebrating his decision to run for mayor of New York City. Though the wounds inflicted were superficial and his wife declined to press charges, Mailer was confined to the mental ward of Bellevue Hospital for seventeen days. Many people assumed—no doubt with good cause—that the whole affair was a monstrous example of absurd theory leading to absurd practice. These same people were not amused when Mailer published the following poem in 1962:

> So long
>   as
>   you
>   use
>   a knife,

there's
some
love
left.[7]

Nor were they delighted by the appearance of *An American Dream* (1965), a novel in which Mailer's hero strangles his wife and manages to avoid prosecution. By the middle of the 1960s, Mailer had pretty well established himself as the most notorious literary figure in America.

This reputation was strengthened throughout the 1960s as Mailer's name appeared again and again in semilurid headlines. In 1962 Mailer and Adele Morales were divorced and Mailer married Lady Jeanne Campbell, the daughter of the Duke of Argyll and the granddaughter of Lord Beaverbrook. One year later Mailer and Lady Campbell were divorced and Mailer married the actress Beverly Bentley. During this obviously hectic period Mailer also published a book in which he lectured John Kennedy on his presidential responsibilities, engaged in a series of barroom brawls which inevitably made the tabloids, and got himself tried—but not convicted—for resisting arrest in Provincetown, Massachusetts. These events were followed, several years later, by his rather more famous arrest at the Pentagon during the antiwar demonstrations of October, 1967. It was after his release at this time that Mailer went on national television and exchanged obscenities with Dick Cavett's audience. Indeed, the late 1960s found Mailer a regular guest on late night talk-shows, where he was usually cast as an American Brendan Behan.[8]

Given Mailer's domestic and public problems during the 1960s, it is remarkable that this period remains the most productive of his career. Amidst what appears to have been personal chaos, Mailer managed to publish one volume of poems, *Deaths for the Ladies (and other disasters)* (1962); two miscellanies, *The Presidential Papers* (1963) and *Cannibals and Christians* (1966); and two novels, *An American Dream* (1965) and *Why Are We in Vietnam?* (1967). At the same time he completed one play, *The Deer Park* (1967), and three movies, *Wild 90* (1967), *Beyond the Law* (1967), and *Maidstone* (1968). Most importantly for him, in 1968 Mailer published two works of nonfiction (*The Armies of the Night* and *Miami and the Siege of Chicago*) which restored the literary reputation he first commanded twenty years earlier. When *The Armies of the Night* won both a

Pulitzer Prize and a National Book Award, Mailer achieved what must have seemed a literary vindication—however temporary.

Since 1968 Mailer has occupied a more respectable position in both American society and American letters than at any time since the publication of his first novel. His activities have remained controversial but much less so than during his "White Negro" period. Mailer's changing attitudes have no doubt been crucial to this transformation. Since 1965 he has grown increasingly suspicious of violence as a means of personal or collective salvation; indeed, he has grown increasingly conservative about life in general. By 1969 Mailer had become sufficiently respectable to run for mayor of New York City in a more or less serious manner, finishing fourth in a field of five candidates in the Democratic primary.[9] His more recent love affairs have generated none of the massive publicity attending his previous marriages. It is easy to exaggerate this newly won "respectability," of course, for Mailer has been involved in many local controversies during the last ten years, including his public quarrel with Women's Liberation, his endorsement of a so-called Fifth Estate, or civilian FBI, to watch over governmental agencies, and his million-dollar contract with Little, Brown.[10] There has been just enough bad publicity to justify Mailer's recent remark that he is the second most unpopular man in America (Richard Nixon ranking first).[11] Increasingly, however, Mailer has been perceived as a serious writer first and an eccentric second, thus reversing his public image from the early 1960s.

Mailer has characterized the last ten years as "a period when, with every thought of beginning a certain big novel which had been promised for a long time, the moot desire to have one's immediate say on contemporary matters kept diverting the novelistic impulse into journalism."[12] These "contemporary matters" have ranged from America's space program to graffiti, from the women's movement to Muhammad Ali. Mailer's recent books on these subjects have kept his name before the public as an inveterate critic of the national scene. The personal revelations occasionally offered in such works should not seduce us into reading them as "autobiographical." As I will argue in later chapters, Mailer's nonfiction describes his own experience of various American phenomena in order to get at the real meaning of recent American history, not to offer a stylized form of public confession. In such recent works as *Of a Fire on the Moon* (1970), *The Prisoner of Sex* (1971), *Marilyn* (1973), and *Genius and*

Lust (1976), Mailer has fleshed out the most attractive side to his public "legend," that of prophetic national commentator.

It would seem that Mailer is a bit skeptical about his recent role, however, for in the passage quoted above he speaks of how his novelistic impulse had been *diverted* into journalism. This should remind us that at the present time Mailer is at work on a long and rather mysterious novel which he hopes will be the capstone to his erratic career.[13] Indeed, by the time these words are in print Mailer may already have begun to publish the first installments of this enormous work. But whether or not it justifies his publisher's million-dollar gamble, Mailer's subsequent work should not deter us from trying to understand and evaluate what he has already done. After all, Mailer's career now spans three decades and more than twenty volumes. These books, though full of personal lore for those interested in Mailer's life, are surely more valuable as evidence of Mailer's continuing effort to win approval as *the* American writer in the postwar period.

It is time we turned to this evidence, especially to those works I consider to be Mailer's most impressive individual achievements: *The Naked and the Dead, The Deer Park,* and *The Armies of the Night*. In analyzing these books and the rest of Mailer's *ouevre*, I cannot hope to do full justice to Mailer as man and legend. However, I do hope to show why the man and his legend are of more than passing interest in the first place.

CHAPTER 2

The Naked and the Dead: *The Beast and the Seer in Man*

IT is often a shock to reread the early work of a writer we have come to admire. The second time around this work usually seems rather thin; we find we have remembered effects which do not exist, values which were never there. Mailer's first novel, *The Naked and the Dead* (1948), is a special example of this phenomenon. To reread Mailer's book is indeed to revise our first impression of it—but in this case the "revision" is all to Mailer's benefit. What we encounter is a work of enduring power, a power which is simply incommensurate with the novel's reputation. We find we have tended to value Mailer's first novel for the wrong reasons: as a guide to combat during World War II, as a work of social criticism, as the best of our recent war novels. *The Naked and the Dead* is all of these things, but it is also something quite different and more important. At the age of twenty-five, Mailer was able to use his military experience as the backbone of a long and complex narrative which transcends limits we usually have in mind in thinking of "war novels." Thirty years later, the nature of this achievement is still not generally recognized.

Certainly *The Naked and the Dead* is more than the "report" of a sensitive young man who survived active service and returned to tell the tale. Mailer began to plan his novel long before his combat experience at Leyte and Luzon. He has traced its origins to the first days of our participation in World War II: "I may as well confess that by December 8th or 9th of 1941, in the forty-eight hours after Pearl Harbor, while worthy young men were wondering where they could be of aid to the war effort, and practical young men were deciding which branch of service was the surest for landing a safe commission, I was worrying darkly whether it would be more likely that a great war novel would be written about Europe or the Pacific . . ." (*Adv*, 28). Much as his General Cummings plans the campaign of Anopopei,

25

Mailer at nineteen was already formulating his strategy for a major novel. He had gone a long way toward fulfilling his ambition before serving a day in the army. While still a student at Harvard, he wrote a short novel which can only be considered a trial run for *The Naked and the Dead*.[1] From books published during the war, especially John Hersey's *Into the Valley* and Harry Brown's *A Walk in the Sun*, he got the idea of writing his novel about a long patrol. In fact, it was this decision which led Mailer to volunteer for service in a reconnaissance outfit.[2] These facts suggest that Mailer went to war in search of combat experience which would enable him to complete a novel he had already conceived. It would be foolish to deny the impact of World War II on the book Mailer finally published, but *The Naked and the Dead* is hardly a transcription of those experiences which came Mailer's way during the war. He seems to have decided rather early that the war could furnish him with an invaluable *background* for a major novel. His preparation for this work covered a full six years.

Discharged in 1946, Mailer began his book in earnest and saw it published in 1948. From the first it was an enormous popular and critical success.[3] Much as his novel was liked, however, Mailer was not given sufficient credit for his *novelistic* abilities. Reviewers tended to assess the book either as a disguised documentary or a work of social criticism. To discuss the novel in such terms is to minimize Mailer's achievement. It is to overlook what differentiates *The Naked and the Dead* from other novels of World War II, novels so different as *The Gallery*, *The Thin Red Line*, and *Catch-22*. What these novels all lack—and what Mailer's reviewers and subsequent critics have failed to perceive in *The Naked and the Dead*—is a dramatic action of such depth and innovative function as to unify all the novel's diverse materials. Features of Mailer's book suggest the documentary, or the work of social criticism, but these features are integrated within the novel's structure and are not its *raison d'etre*. To establish this point is a first step toward clarifying the real achievement of Mailer's "war novel."

I   *The Novel as Documentary*

The uncritical reader of Mailer's first novel would take it to be a disguised documentary. Many critics have, in fact, assumed that Mailer set out to transcribe the crucial events of his army career. Thus we have Marvin Mudrick's description of the novel as "a manual of soldiering in the tropics."[4] Thus we have Ira Wolfert's opinion that in *The Naked and the Dead* "the most powerful talents developed . . . are those of the journalist. The story is reported. It is not so much a reading of life as a description in depth of an event in life."[5]

Such views may appear reductive, but who would deny that Mailer's concern for verisimilitude often seems obsessive? The intricacies of davit machinery; the mechanics of tent building; the aspect of a rotting corpse; the effects of a long, sustained march through jungle—almost everything in the novel is rendered in elaborate, professional detail, as Mailer follows an army platoon through the stages of a Pacific campaign. Nor is this merely a matter of itemizing the paraphernalia of army life. Repeatedly Mailer employs his "phenomenal talent for recording the precise look and feel of things"[6] to illumine the conditions his characters must suffer. Nor is he less convincing when dealing with his fictional campaign as a whole. When looking over the shoulder of General Cummings and analyzing the progress of the campaign, Mailer achieves the authority of a retired army officer dictating his memoirs.

But of course Mailer is not dictating memoirs, his own or his characters'. While many of the novel's episodes derive from his personal experiences, Mailer has all but told us that we should not read the book in this fashion: "In the author's eyes, *The Naked and the Dead* is not a realistic documentary; it is, rather, a symbolic book, of which the theme is the conflict between the beast and the seer in man. The number of events experienced by the one platoon couldn't possibly have happened to any one army platoon in the war, but represent a composite view of the Pacific war."[7] Mailer would not deny that his work is realistic; he has also said that "the book will stand or fall as a realistic novel."[8] What he *would* deny is an interpretation of a part as the whole, the techniques of a novel as denoting its formal ends. Technically speaking, Mailer has adopted the realistic conventions of most twentieth-century American fiction. But realistic techniques do not point unerringly to the formal aims of a "realistic documentary." Besides referring to *The Naked and the Dead* as a "symbolic" book, Mailer has insisted that he is neither a realist nor a naturalist: "That terrible word 'naturalism.' It was my literary heritage—the things I learned from Dos Passos and Farrell. I took naturally to it, that's the way one wrote a book. But I really was off on a mystic kick. Actually—a funny thing—the biggest influence on

Naked was *Moby Dick*."[9] A book whose aspirations suggest those of *Moby-Dick* should not be discussed as a documentary, "realistic" or otherwise.

The novel's symbolism is one feature which transcends the limits of a documentary, but more important still is the story told. Some of the enormous detail in this book may be attributed to Mailer's indulgence of his special knowledge of war; certain episodes and characters contribute little except insofar as they add to Mailer's "description in depth of an event in life." But Mailer usually manages to involve whatever he describes in his elaboration of a full-scale dramatic action. The conditions on Anopopei, Mailer's mythical Pacific island; the routine of army life; the many actions forced upon the men— these things are always seen in relation to the characters themselves with their developing conflicts. This makes all the difference in how we respond to the novel. Contrast the effect of *The Naked and the Dead* with that of James Jones' *The Thin Red Line* (1962), a novel which might truly be called a realistic documentary.

The Thin Red Line resembles Mailer's novel in many obvious ways. It too describes the campaign for possession of a single Pacific island (in this case, Guadalcanal). Like Mailer, Jones observes every facet of the campaign from the landing to the mopping up. Like Mailer again, Jones employs the literary device of the "microcosm" when he follows a representative group of men (C-for-Charley Company) throughout the campaign. Yet the two books aren't really similar, as Mailer has himself remarked. He has aptly described *The Thin Red Line* as "so broad and true a portrait of combat that it could be used as a textbook at the Infantry School if the Army is any less chicken than it used to be." He has gone to the heart of Jones' intentions: "Jones' aim, after all, is not to create character but the feel of combat, the psychology of men." For Mailer, "*The Naked and the Dead* is concerned more with characters than military action"; so he cannot see that his book is truly comparable to *The Thin Red Line* (*CC*, 112).

Mailer's comments are very much to the point. His novel differs from Jones' in that its central concern is to develop its many characters. Jones' "characters" might as well go unnamed, so little difference does it make who they are or what they do in the book except at the moment when Jones happens to use them to illustrate an aspect of combat. There is nothing in *The Thin Red Line* comparable to Mailer's gradual development of the conflicts among his major characters. There is no effort to prepare for shifts in the action, as is the case throughout *The Naked and the Dead*. In fact, there is no dramatic action in *The Thin Red Line*. As Mailer suggests, Jones wasn't interested in such an action; his intentions actually correspond to those Mudrick and Wolfert attribute to Mailer. *The Naked and the Dead*, on the other hand, is rooted in the traditional development of character through a structured series of episodes. We must judge its documentary features as they do or do not serve in this development.

II   *The Novel as Social Critique*

Much of the same argument applies to elements of social criticism in *The Naked and the Dead*. The existence of such elements is obvious: the criticism of the army as an institution which informs every incident in the novel; the attack on totalitarianism which emerges from the discussions between General Cummings and his aide, Lieutenant Hearn; the portrait of American society developed through the I and R platoon, especially in the "Time Machine" biographies of eight enlisted men and two officers (Cummings and Hearn). Yet we must still ask how these elements function in the novel as a whole.

Before we assess its function, however, we should first understand the *nature* of Mailer's social criticism. Far too often *The Naked and the Dead* has been treated as the work of a "young liberal" whose critique of American society is substantially the same as that of Dos Passos, Farrell, and Steinbeck.[10] Now it is true that prior to World War II Mailer was, in his own words, a "progressive-liberal." And in 1948, *after* finishing *The Naked and the Dead* and travelling through Europe, Mailer did join the campaign for Henry Wallace. Nonetheless, *The Naked and the Dead* is not the work of a political liberal. In *Advertisements for Myself*, Mailer suggests that his early short novel, "A Calculus at Heaven," makes "an interesting contrast to *The Naked and the Dead*, for it is an attempt of the imagination (aided and warped by books, movies, war correspondents, and the liberal mentality) to guess what war might really be like" (*Adv*, 28). "A Calculus at Heaven" is determined in part by "the liberal mentality," and *therefore* it makes an interesting *contrast* to *The Naked and the Dead*. If this seems to press very hard on Mailer's meaning, we have his own word for it that when he wrote his first novel he was an anarchist, not a liberal (*Adv*, 271).

This helps to explain some common misreadings of the book. Standard critical procedure has gone something like this: first, the critic has assumed that *The Naked and the Dead* is a thesis novel;

second, he has assumed that its thesis resembles the sort we find in a
writer like Dos Passos, for Mailer's "sympathies" are also progressive;
third, he has found that the novel's action does not consistently
support the presumed liberal thesis; and so fourth, he either has
pointed out Mailer's failures of execution or begun to talk about
trusting the tale and not the teller.[11] This procedure involves at least
two fallacies: that *The Naked and the Dead* is a thesis novel; that
Mailer uses the book to embody liberal values and a liberal social
critique. I will return to these problems after considering the novel's
action, where I hope to show that what seems "inconsistent" or
"weak" to a reader who takes Mailer's liberalism for granted is
nothing of the sort if we approach the novel without this presupposi-
tion. Here, however, I would stress the point that Mailer's novel was
not written to do the work of a sociologist.

Mailer's social vision does emerge in the course of his novel,
especially in those sections where he reveals the backgrounds of his
characters. But *The Naked and the Dead* doesn't exist for the sake of
this vision; Mailer's characters are not "examples" in a sociological
tract. Consider the "Time Machine" sections. If *The Naked and the
Dead* were really a thesis novel, these biographies would function as
evidence in Mailer's "argument" concerning the American social
scene; but I think Barry Leeds has suggested the real relation
between the biographies and the rest of the novel:

> Thus, while *The Time Machine* is used to portray the home of a Midwestern
> businessman, the slums of Boston, or Harvard Yard, it is the presence on
> Anopopei of men who have experienced these places, which justifies Mailer's
> detailed treatment of them, and obviates the possibility of their introduction
> seeming stilted. Every element of American society dealt with becomes
> integral to the novel as a whole, not merely because it seems to fit into a
> re-creation of that society, but because it is drawn from the life of a character
> in whom the reader has come to believe.[12]

The "Time Machine" may be a laborious device for enriching our
experience with the men on Anopopei, but that is its function. Leeds
cites Martinez, but he might have mentioned any of a number of
characters. Another example should clarify his point. When he learns
of his wife's death, Gallagher becomes for the first time of some
importance in the novel. At this point Mailer introduces a "Time
Machine" section on Gallagher's Boston-Irish background, his training in frustrated prejudice (266-79).[13] Just when we can see Gallagher
as fully human, stunned by the loss of his wife, Mailer chooses to

highlight his ignorance and bigotry. Paradoxically, we are all the more impressed by Gallagher's intense feeling for his wife. He becomes a more complex and interesting character than would have been possible if either his biography or his mourning had been presented independently. Thus Mailer uses the "Time Machine" to illuminate character, introducing the device at just that moment in the narrative when it can best supplement the novel's action.

The "Time Machine" differs, then, from similar devices in the works of John Dos Passos.[14] The Camera Eye, Newsreel, and biography sections in *U.S.A.*, for example, are clearly intended to complement the narrative in the manner of a thesis novel. These sections aren't directly related to the narrative; they don't even concern its characters. Instead, they are determined by and substantiate Dos Passos' attack on the American social system. Mailer's use of a similar device is for a quite different end. The "Time Machine" sections are not just thematically related to the narrative; they are intended to comment on each character's role in the action. When this doesn't happen—as in the belated "Time Machine" passage devoted to Polack, a figure of no real significance in the novel (608-20)—the reader is likely to find the "Time Machine" material digressive, even intrusive. Mailer's novel differs from Dos Passos' trilogy in its use of social elements to clarify a dramatic action, not a social argument.

III   *The Novel as Dramatic Action*

What I am suggesting is that *The Naked and the Dead* is a rather traditional novel. This is not meant as a criticism of the book. If it lacks the stylistic and formal innovations of Mailer's more recent novels, *An American Dream* (1965) and *Why Are We in Vietnam?* (1967), *The Naked and the Dead* is nonetheless a more successful work. It is successful in its adaptation of a novelistic form traceable from Richardson and Fielding down to Mailer's immediate precursors, Hemingway and Faulkner. This form emphasizes character and action—staples of fiction which are as central to *The Naked and the Dead* as they are to the novels of Austen and Dickens. Interpretation of the work should begin with precisely these elements.

It may seem rather harmless to argue that *The Naked and the Dead* is essentially "a novel of character," as John Aldridge first suggested and as Mailer has confirmed.[15] In fact, however, there are fairly important consequences if we accept this idea. Indeed, we will probably have to reject the more popular interpretations of the novel. Consider a specific issue, concerning the novel's ending. In a recent critique, Randall Waldron has argued the "case" against Mailer's conclusion:

> The central conflict in *The Naked and the Dead* is between the mechanistic forces of "the system" and the will to individual integrity. Commanding General Cummings, brilliant and ruthless evangel of fascist power and control, and iron-handed, hard-nosed Sergeant Croft personify the machine. Opposing them in the attempt to maintain personal dignity and identity are Cummings' confused young aide, Lieutenant Hearn, and Private Valsen, rebellious member of Croft's platoon. Mailer fails to bring this conflict to any satisfying resolution: at the novel's end Hearn is dead and Valsen's stubborn pride defeated, but likewise Croft is beaten and humiliated and Cummings' personal ambitions thwarted . . . . the conclusion of *The Naked and the Dead* and its total meaning are unclear.[16]

Waldron dislikes the novel's conclusion for the same reason as Norman Podhoretz and John Aldridge: Mailer's ending fails to generate the radical "protest" he presumably intended.[17] Waldron obviously expects the book to end as this kind of thesis novel is supposed to end—with a clear demarcation between victim and victimizer. Like Podhoretz and Aldridge, he assumes that Mailer conceived the book as a warning against totalitarian tendencies in America; like these critics, he cannot see that Mailer achieves this purpose by treating his villains in the same manner as his heroes.

But why should we assume that Mailer intended to write a protest novel? If we make this assumption, the novel's ending—indeed, the coherence of the whole work—is called into question. We would at least expect Mailer to distinguish sufficiently among his characters to clarify his own moral position and articulate his "warning." As Waldron remarks, Mailer has "failed" to do this. My own view is that he never intended to do so. If we stop treating Cummings, Croft, Hearn, and Valsen as representative figures in a political allegory, we should come to see that Mailer has prepared all along for the ending Waldron and the others find so disappointing. In examining the novel as a dramatic action, we should not only make sense of what others have found "unclear"; we should also get at the true sources of its power.

Mailer's published remarks on the composition of his novel tend to confirm that it wasn't organized around a political or social "thesis." Mailer has said from the first that he wanted to structure his novel around a long patrol involving a single army platoon.[18] It seems likely that he first intended to write a collective novel in the manner of Dos Passos, using the patrol to examine under stress a group of men broadly representative of American society. While he does do something like this in the published novel, Mailer has revealed that his book changed during the writing of its second draft. It changed because he chose to develop two characters outside the platoon, General Cummings and Lieutenant Hearn: "The part about the platoon went well from the beginning, but the Lieutenant and the General in the first draft were stock characters. If it had been published at that point the book would have been considered an interesting war novel with some good scenes, no more. The second draft was the bonus. Cummings and Hearn were done in the second draft."[19] As Mailer suggests, it was the fleshing out of Cummings and Hearn which "made" his novel as a work of art. Mailer patterned their relationship after the conflict between Croft and Valsen, the leading members of the platoon and presumably the main characters in his initial draft. *The Naked and the Dead* came more and more to deal with these four major figures; it began to take on the full dimensions of a novel of character.

Mailer's two plot lines resemble each other so, they might almost be considered a double plot. The basic resemblance between the two feuds (Cummings vs. Hearn, Croft vs. Valsen) is fairly obvious. In each case a character of liberal sympathies fights for his integrity against a fascistic superior; each of the "good" characters is defeated, while each "bad" character fails in his most ambitious undertaking. Croft's tactics against Valsen are openly sadistic, whereas Cummings exercises an intellectual tyranny over Hearn; but finally this is a minor distinction, for the results are indistinguishable. These conflicts are reminiscent of much of the "protest" literature to which *The Naked and the Dead* has been compared. Cummings and Croft seem prototype fascists, the "villains" of a hundred proletarian novels; Hearn and Valsen seem the archetypal "victims" of such novels. If we take a closer look, however, we should discover subtleties which are appropriate to Mailer's overall design.

Initially the feud between Croft and Valsen seems a simple matter of irreconcilable personalities. Certainly this is our impression in part one, where Croft and Valsen nearly come to blows in a scene which is repeated with variations throughout the novel, until their quarrel is resolved on Mount Anaka. Their "roles" are fixed this early: Croft as the aggressive platoon leader, Red as the recalcitrant private who

resists authority and authoritarians (31–32). Red is presented from
the outset as a proud but rather ineffectual man who is capable of
feeling "a sad compassion in which one seems to understand everything, all that men want and fail to get" (14), but who has no hope of
translating his feelings into action: "Everything is crapped up,
everything is phony, everything curdles when you touch it" (350).
Both his compassion for others and his personal cynicism define Red
as Croft's opposite number. Croft is an obvious, even a spectacular
sadist. As a National Guardsman, he kills a striker for no other reason
than the pleasure it gives him (161). On Anopopei he tantalizes a
Japanese prisoner with kindness before shooting him in the head (195),
crushes a small bird in his bare hand (530), and coldly arranges the
death of Hearn (598). Croft loves combat, for only in combat does he
find release from his hatred of the world (his "Time Machine" section
concludes, "I HATE EVERYTHING WHICH IS NOT IN
MYSELF"—p. 164). Croft must master everything which is not in
himself. He is confident that he can do so, for "he had a deep
unspoken belief that whatever made things happen was on his side"
(9).

Yet Croft and Valsen are not mere foils, as Mailer reveals in the
first half of part two. This section of the novel moves toward two
separate "moments of truth," one experienced by Croft and the other
by Valsen. The first such moment climaxes Mailer's account of the
Japanese counterattack, a performance as fine as anything in the
book. Here we see Croft in his natural element, the violence of war.
He is shown controlling his men so fiercely that he revives Valsen's
hatred (125, 129); he is shown coming down on weakness as if it were a
personal enemy (137). Yet the climax of this episode is Croft's
moment of *fear*, more precisely his awareness that he too can be made
afraid. This sends "a terrible rage working through his weary body"
(155), and its effects are felt through the rest of the novel, until Croft's
rage is expended against Mount Anaka.

The second climactic "moment" occurs when the men go to search
Japanese bodies for souvenirs. This hunt is a nightmare, revealing, in
Chester Eisinger's words, "the deepest urge toward violence and
debasement in human beings."[20] Red finds it oppressive because he
must pass through piles of rotting bodies. The stench is overpower-
ing, the corpses horribly distorted and maggot-ridden. Suddenly,
Red is "sober and very weary." Unlike the others, Red is aware that
he is surrounded by the bodies of *men*. Standing over one such body,
he experiences a kind of epiphany: "Very deep inside himself he was

thinking that this was a man who had once wanted things, and the thought of his own death was always a little unbelievable to him. The man had had a childhood, a youth and a young manhood, and there had been dreams and memories. Red was realizing with surprise and shock, as if he were looking at a corpse for the first time, that a man was really a very fragile thing" (216). Different as Croft and Valsen are, their climactic insights in part two are quite similar. Each discovers that "a man was really a very fragile thing." They differ of course in how they respond to this discovery. Croft tries to exorcise it through violence, while Red accepts it with a "wise" melancholy. This section of the book is structured so as to reveal the common anxieties underlying their radically different approaches to life.

In the second half of part two, Mailer develops an even more complex antagonism. Prior to the represented action, Cummings has more or less adopted Hearn as his protege. He has seen in Hearn an intellectual equal and a sympathetic ear for his theories on the nature of power. When Hearn responds to the general's attentions with something less than gratitude, his fate is to illustrate Cummings' first principle: " 'There's one thing about power. It can flow only from the top down. When there are little surges of resistance at the middle levels, it merely calls for more power to be directed downward, to burn it out' " (323). Throughout the book we see Cummings trying to do just this, to "burn out" Hearn's resistance. The conflict here seems quite straightforward. Indeed, critics often refer to Hearn as Mailer's liberal spokesman. Hearn's resistance to Cummings is supposed to represent Mailer's own political feelings and to justify his role as the novel's "hero."

The problem is that Hearn does not so much represent liberalism as the *desire* to be liberal. Surely he is an odd humanitarian: he likes few people (69, 328), he is a self-confessed snob (78), he feels distaste for Jews (83) and a "trace of contempt" for the enlisted man (168). Temperamentally, Hearn is an artistocrat. It isn't surprising that he defends his liberal notions with faint conviction, for his real commitment is to himself: "The only thing that had been important was to let no one in any ultimate issue ever violate your integrity" (326). Hearn would protect his "inviolate freedom" and so avoid "all the wants and sores that caught up everybody about him" (79). His motto is appropriately sterile: "The only thing to do is to get by on style" (326). Defined by his detachment, his distance from real human concerns, Hearn is known by his failures to act.

Because he feels no real commitment to his humanitarian interests,

Hearn is vulnerable to the same urges which move Cummings and Croft. Hearn is fascinated by Cummings, who has the ability "to extend his thoughts into immediate and effective action" (77), because Hearn is drawn to power himself: "Always there was the power that leaped at you, invited you" (353). Resentment of his position vis-a-vis Cummings is matched by his desire to be like Cummings: ". . . he had acquiesced in the dog-role, had even had the dog's dream, carefully submerged, of someday equaling the master" (313). Hearn comes to believe that "divorced of all the environmental trappings, all the confused and misleading attitudes he had absorbed, he was basically like Cummings" (392). He even comes to fear that "when he searched himself he was just another Croft" (580).

What Hearn fears is that he is no less a fascist than Cummings or Croft. But even Cummings is more complex than this might suggest. A self-styled "reactionary," Cummings prefers fascism to communism because "it's grounded firmly in men's actual natures" (321). To say the least, Cummings has no high opinion of man's nature. He thinks Hitler "the interpreter of twentieth-century man" and believes " 'there's never a man who can swear to his own innocence. We're all guilty, that's the truth' " (313). But of course Cummings doesn't see himself as he sees other men. Indeed, he has a mystical sense of his own destiny: " 'The fact that you're holding the gun and the other man is not is no accident. It's a product of everything you've achieved, it assumes that you're . . . you're aware enough, you have the gun when you need it' " (83–84). Cummings views himself as the man with the gun. He is speaking of himself, not "man," when he says that "man is in transit between brute and God" (323).

Cummings' vanity is immense, his ambitions worthy of Ahab. We learn early that his intention on Anopopei is to "mold" his troops, the terrain, and even "the circuits of chance" to the contours of his will (85). Confident that he can dispose of any obstacle, natural or human, Cummings believes that life is like a game of chess (180). But his rationality is a disguise, as Mailer makes clear by revealing the real forces at work on Cummings: self-pity amounting to paranoia, and latent homosexuality.[21] As the novel unfolds, we learn that Cummings is no exception to his own dictum on the nature of man. His cool outward appearance is a "facade" which can be stripped away to reveal "a naked animal closeted with its bone" (77). Ultimately, Cummings is no closer to harmonizing "Plant and Phantom,"[22] body and spirit, than are the men of Croft's platoon, or Hearn.

During part two, then, we come to see the novel's central conflicts as rather more ambiguous than they at first appeared; in each case the antagonists have more in common than we might have supposed. This is made especially clear in part three, where the four major figures all suffer a remarkably similar fate. I have already noted that each of the "good" characters is defeated by his totalitarian opponent. Hearn is the victim of both Cummings and Croft, for Cummings transfers Hearn into a platoon already selected for a dangerous mission and Croft deliberately plots his death. Red's defeat isn't fatal, but it is no less decisive. A man committed to nothing except his own personal integrity, Red is so beaten down that he is finally *relieved* when he confronts Croft and is defeated: "At the base of his shame was an added guilt. He was glad it was over, glad the long contest with Croft was finished, and he could obey orders with submission, without feeling that he must resist" (696).

Yet if they triumph over Hearn and Valsen, Cummings and Croft are hardly the novel's "victors." Throughout part three Croft's efforts are directed toward conquering Mount Anaka, the great mountain that towers over Anopopei, "taunting" Croft with its "purity" and "austerity" (497, 522, 527). The mountain becomes for Croft what his troops are for Cummings: the "other" which because it resists his control must be molded to serve his will. Like Cummings, however, Croft is unable to control the circuits of chance. When he stumbles over a hornets' nest, the men flee down the mountain and the march is abruptly ended (699–700). Croft is left puzzled and spent: "Croft kept looking at the mountain. He had lost it, had missed some tantalizing revelation of himself. Of himself and much more. Of life. Everything" (709). This passage recalls the single section devoted to Cummings in part three. Faced with the "mass inertia or the inertia of the masses," the men's resistance to his more grandiose ambitions, Cummings is unable to find a meaningful pattern among the forces at work in the campaign: "There was order but he could not reduce it to the form of a single curve. Things eluded him" (571). Like Croft, Cummings must finally give the circuits of chance their due. He attempts with his final attack what Croft attempts on Mount Anaka, but the campaign ends in a manner he could never have anticipated (Major Dalleson, not Cummings, engineers the final assault). Cummings is forced to admit that "he had had very little or perhaps nothing at all to do with this victory, or indeed any victory" (716). For Cummings, too, there comes the knowledge of personal limitation.

As remarked earlier, Mailer has been criticized for refusing to create ideologically satisfying fates for his characters, as would be necessary if he were to achieve a radical "protest." The assumption here is that Mailer wrote his book to "defend liberalism,"[23] to warn against the antiliberal forces within the American system. But Mailer has instead made it clear that he "intended" something quite different—something which might even *require* the treatment of character we find in *The Naked and the Dead*. Mailer has said that he conceived the novel as "a parable about the movement of man through history";[24] he has defined its basic theme as "the conflict between the beast and the seer in man."[25] It would seem that for Mailer the movement of man through history is an ongoing struggle between the bestial and visionary forces in man himself. This idea isn't terribly original, of course, but the power of *The Naked and the Dead* doesn't depend on the originality of its ideas. It is a question of how well they are embodied in the novel's characters and events.

Besides, Mailer's ideas are not so schematic as I may have suggested. Unlike the typical proletarian or social novel, *The Naked and the Dead* does not present its beasts and seers in obvious counterpoint. If Croft is set against Valsen in the book, who is the beast and who is the seer? The epigraph to part three is relevant here: "Even the wisest among you is only a disharmony and hybrid of plant and phantom. But do I bid you become phantoms and plants?" (431).[26] This rhetorical question implies that man should be neither "plant" nor "phantom" exclusively; neither all body nor all soul; neither beast nor seer. Man should achieve a harmony between the physical and the spiritual, though, as Nietzsche observes, even the wisest among us is a "disharmony and hybrid." This is certainly true of the major figures in *The Naked and the Dead*, each of whom carries within himself the bestial and visionary forces Nietzsche refers to. The ultimate effect of Mailer's parallel plots is to emphasize this "disharmony" in each character. When Cummings and Croft suffer defeats comparable to those of Hearn and Valsen, we should realize that Mailer has rejected a crude contrast between "good" and "evil." In dramatizing the conflict between the beast and the seer in man, Mailer has shown that *all* of his characters are subject to the same conflict.[27]

Mailer has surely established this kinship between Cummings and Croft. These men resemble each other in many obvious ways. They are both power moralists who rely on fear and hatred in their command of others; they are both inordinately ambitious; they both function as Hearn's enemy and plan to have him killed. Each is "coldly efficient" (179), latently homosexual,[28] and obsessed with his wife's infidelity (182, 200). They share an extreme individualism which is coupled with a strong sense of personal destiny. Whereas Cummings believes "the fact that you're holding the gun and the other man is not is no accident," Croft believes that "if a man gets wounded, it's his own goddam fault" (522)—if Cummings sees himself as the man with the gun, Croft sees himself as the man who will never be wounded. Cummings and Croft are most alike in their rejection of accident or chance as a determining force in life. We have seen that Cummings' ambition is nothing less than to mold the circuits of chance, while Croft has "a deep unspoken belief that whatever made things happen was on his side." Each has a naive faith that he can work his will on the world.

In their rejection of determinism, Cummings and Croft almost justify Podhoretz' suggestion that they are the novel's "natural heroes."[29] While Hearn and Valsen suggest vacillation and futility, Cummings and Croft are all energy and commitment. "Natural heroes" is a bit much, however. It is essential that we not see Cummings and Croft as mere villains, but we should not equate Mailer's admiration for certain qualities in Croft, say, with admiration for the character as a whole.[30] In response to the question "Whom do you hate?" Mailer has answered, "People who have power and no compassion, that is, no simple human understanding" (*Adv*, 271). Can we fail to apply this statement to Cummings and Croft?

What prevents these characters from being purely hateful is what Mailer calls their "vision." Croft is inspired by a "crude unformed vision" (156), and Cummings is driven by "one great vision" (323), momentarily embodied when he observes his first battlefield and experiences "the largest vision that has ever entered his soul": "There were all those men, and there had been someone above them, ordering them, changing perhaps forever the fiber of their lives. . . . *There were things one could do.*" As he surveys the battlefield, Cummings is "choked with the intensity of his emotion, the rage, the undefined and mighty hunger" (415). This hunger is Croft's crude unformed vision; this rage is Croft's "rage" at the frustrations of the final patrol (527). Moreover, the vision these men share is no mean one. Cummings' greatest urge is for omnipotence, as we have seen; and Croft is tantalized by "vistas of such omnipotence he must wonder at his own audacity" (40). The common spirit which links Cummings and Croft is unmistakable. In one sense they are the novel's "seers": confident of the world's tractability, they are determined to achieve destinies commensurate with their mighty hunger.

Unfortunately, Cummings and Croft are also the novel's principal "beasts." There is nothing so despicable in *The Naked and the Dead* as Croft's calculated destruction of the lame bird discovered by one of his men; and Cummings is subject to the same impulses, as we learn when he comes upon a cigarette Hearn had put out on his floor: "If he had been holding an animal in his hands at that instant he would have strangled it" (318). Hearn discovers early in the book that Cummings is capable of atrocities as great as any Croft will later commit. Behind the general's facade is that naked animal closeted with its bone. It is the naked animal in Cummings which finds expression in his power morality, his persecution and finally his execution of Hearn.[31] The conflict between the beast and the seer in man is precisely the conflict within both Cummings and Croft. The urges which move them are *both* bestial and visionary.

In his portraits of Hearn and Valsen, Mailer further undermines the "structure of protest"[32] readers have expected of him. To achieve such "protest," Mailer would have had to depict Hearn and Valsen as more or less admirable figures victimized by the representatives of an unjust society; but of course they are presented quite differently. Whereas Cummings believes that "in the Army the idea of individual personality is just a hindrance" (180–81), Hearn and Valsen have no commitment *except* to their individual personalities. Both place the highest value on what Hearn calls "inviolate freedom." They ask nothing more specific from life because they also share contempt for what life offers: Red's "particular blend of pessimism and fatalism" (444) is everywhere evident, while Hearn believes that "if you searched something long enough, it always turned to dirt" (183). Because they have found so little to value in life, Hearn and Valsen have lived as drifters. Unlike Red, Hearn hasn't literally been a hobo, but his life style might easily be mistaken for Valsen's: "Get potted, get screwed, and get up in the morning, somehow" (347). Hearn and Valsen are confirmed in their pessimism by what happens to them on Anopopei. Each is made to struggle for his inviolate freedom; each comes to the conclusion that "there were no answers" in this struggle (585, 704). The repetition of this exact phrase emphasizes that neither Hearn nor Valsen has been able to discover a sustaining belief. In both men the qualities of the seer have been blunted.

We tend to think of Hearn and Valsen in relation to their enemies, but this contrast can be misleading. If they differ from Cummings and Croft, their crucial weaknesses often remind us of those characters. Hearn discovers in himself many of the qualities which unite

Cummings and Croft. Both Hearn and Cummings are "born in the aristocracy of the wealthy midwestern family" (169); both have domineering fathers who force them into "masculine" activities, Hearn into boys' camps and athletics, Cummings into military school; both become "cold rather than shy" (407) and suffer a displaced sex life (like Cummings, Hearn "fights out battles with himself" upon the bodies of his women—p. 416). During a football game, Hearn experiences "an instant of complete startling gratification when he knew the ball carrier was helpless, waiting to be hit" (344)—a clear enough parallel to Croft's sadism. The connection between Hearn and Croft is most obvious during the patrol, where each man tries to redeem his failure early in the campaign and Hearn comes to think of himself as "another Croft."

While Red does not so clearly resemble Cummings, there are interesting similarities. When the campaign begins to go badly, Cummings undergoes "the amazement and terror of a driver who finds his machine directing itself, starting and halting when *it* desires" (300). This echoes Red's discovery of "a pattern where there shouldn't be one" (39) after the death of a young soldier. Red's kinship with Croft has already been suggested. Once he has been defeated by Croft, Red finds that he is happy to obey orders without feeling he must resist them. When the march up Mount Anaka ends, Croft feels much the same emotion: "Deep inside himself, Croft was relieved that he had not been able to climb the mountain. . . . Croft was rested by the unadmitted knowledge that he had found a limit to his hunger" (701). Once their ambitions are thwarted, Cummings and Croft are seen as not altogether different from even Red Valsen.

Does the resemblance among these characters "humanize" Cummings and Croft or "expose" Hearn and Valsen? The answer must of course be—*both*. Cummings and Croft are not entirely reprehensible; Hearn and Valsen are not quite admirable. The whole action has been directed toward these ironic judgments. "Only connect," Forster advised, but none of the major characters is able to balance the beast and seer within himself, though each shares these qualities in varying degrees. What Red lacks in energy and purpose, Croft lacks in compassion and the ability to expand his unformed vision beyond the need for power. It is much the same with Hearn and Cummings. Hearn would seem the one most likely to connect the warring forces in himself, but Hearn is also perhaps the most incomplete of the major figures. Neither his human sympathy nor desire for power is finally authentic. It is one of the novel's many ironies that Hearn is nonetheless the one character who achieves even a limited dignity.[33] In *The Naked and the Dead* there is no correlation at all between "goodness" and the fruits thereof.

While dramatizing their conflicts, Mailer hints that his characters are basically similar. This doesn't evidence moral or aesthetic confusion; instead, it makes possible Mailer's rather terrible commentary upon his creations. At the end he collapses their several fates into a single fate—disillusionment—and confirms what has been implicit throughout: that man is a "disharmony," "corrupted, confused to the point of helplessness," with the world he inherits having no sympathy for man's weakness. Croft and Valsen may seem polar opposites, but whether they seek power or personal freedom they are doomed to a common failure. Their desires—so apparently different—represent what Mailer once insisted we see in all his characters: "yearnings for a better world."[34] Mailer doesn't mock these desires; they are all there is to redeem Cummings and Croft even slightly. What he does is show how nearly impossible it is to realize such "yearnings."

Mailer does this in a work which engages our feelings in the manner of all great novels. Rather than document the experience of combat or the failure of our political system, Mailer has created a dramatic action which embodies more universal concerns. The result is a dark but moving image of man and his condition. The image is one Mailer will never again so starkly present in his fiction; indeed, it is possible to see all of his subsequent work as an attempt to qualify or even disavow the bleak implications of his first novel. The "truth" of this image is not really in question, however. What counts here is Mailer's success in fleshing out the elaborate dramatic action which unifies his book. A novel of character in the best sense of that phrase, *The Naked and the Dead* remains one of Mailer's most impressive achievements.

CHAPTER 3

The Deer Park: *The Rare Tenderness of Tragedy*

M AILER has expressed pleasure at the authoritative voice he still
hears in *The Naked and the Dead*: ". . . it seems to be at dead
center—'Yes,' it is always saying, 'this is about the way it is.' " He has
also explained how this authority was lost, both in his work and in his
personal life, with the extraordinary success of his first novel:
"Naturally, I was blasted a considerable distance away from dead
center by the size of its success, and I spent the next few years trying
to gobble up the experiences of a victorious man when I was still no
man at all" (*Adv*, 92). Eventually Mailer's biographers will reveal the
important events of this period, the most mysterious in Mailer's
career; but at this point little need be said of the years leading from
the triumph of *The Naked and the Dead* to the miserable failure of
Barbary Shore (1951). Mailer is almost alone in defending his second
novel: ". . . it could be that if my work is alive one hundred years from
now, *Barbary Shore* will be considered the richest of my first three
novels" (*Adv*, 94). But let us hope not. Let us hope instead that in
something less than one hundred years Mailer's third novel, *The
Deer Park* (1955), will be recognized as the book in which he regained
his sense of "the way it is" and gave us one of the best American
novels published since World War II.

For a novel this exceptional, *The Deer Park* was a long time in even
finding a publisher. Mailer has provided a full account of his troubles
with the book, its conception, composition, revision, publication,
and reception. What stands out in this account is that seven
publishing houses refused *The Deer Park* before G. P. Putnam's Sons
accepted it (*Adv*, 231). The source of this hostility was revealed in the
novel's reviews—Mailer's reward for his long and tortured struggle
with *The Deer Park* was to discover that a good many readers thought

43

it a dirty book. Sidney Alexander went so far as to suggest that *The Deer Park* was "not even good pornography," though he did assure us that it *was* pornography: "Norman Mailer's new novel makes one think of a vice-squad man who goes in to investigate and stays to participate."[1] It is hard to understand how a novel so "mild" by contemporary standards could have aroused such alarm. It is amusing to read that Mailer revised *The Deer Park* with the fear of censorship in the back of his mind (*Adv*, 241–42). It is not so amusing to reflect on the fact that a majority of the novel's first critics saw in it little more than a crass preoccupation with sex. Strange that a writer who hates pornography as much as Mailer does should be plagued by the accusation that his own works are obscene.[2]

If *The Deer Park* is not a "sensational" work, a "shocker" in the great tradition of Irving Wallace and Harold Robbins, what then is it? Mailer's critics have tended to classify *The Deer Park* as a "Hollywood novel," much as *The Naked and the Dead* has been labeled a "war novel." Michael Millgate suggests as much in defining "the essential theme" in serious novels about Hollywood: "Reality is distorted, human values are inverted or destroyed, and commercialism is always and everywhere the enemy. This is the essential theme of all serious Hollywood novels. It is at the heart of the struggle between Stahr and Brady in *The Last Tycoon*, between Fineman and Sammy Glick in *What Makes Sammy Run?*, between Halliday and Milgrim in *The Disenchanted*, between Eitel and Teppis in *The Deer Park*."[3] Indeed, Mailer has explained that as he first conceived his book the conflict between Eitel and Teppis was central: "The original title of *The Deer Park* was *The Idol and the Octopus*. The book was going to be about Charles Francis Eitel, the Director, and Herman Teppis, the Producer, and the underlying theme was the war between those who wished to make an idol out of art, the artists, and the patron who sued art for power, the octopus."[4]

This is the book Millgate addresses—the book Mailer *was* going to write but did not. Mailer's success in detailing the world of Hollywood has obscured the fact that his central concern is the love affair between Charley Eitel and Elena Esposito. Mailer has told us that in his final revisions he changed the novel's style to reflect the character of his narrator, Sergius O'Shaugnessy. The result, in Mailer's view, was to transfigure the story told by Sergius. This story is said to involve "two people who are strong as well as weak, corrupt as much as pure" (*Adv*, 238)—Eitel and Elena. As Mailer says elsewhere, *The*

Deer Park is about "a movie director and a girl with whom he had a bad affair" (*Adv*, 242). Its reviewers and critics to the contrary, *The Deer Park* is a love story.

I emphasize this point because critical discussions of the novel tend to focus on Mailer's satirical presentation of Hollywood; to regret the fact that Eitel is the central character;[5] or, as with Millgate, to misrepresent Mailer's interest in Eitel. Each of these tendencies leads us away from Mailer's real achievement. If Eitel was first conceived as a representative artist in dubious battle with the Philistines (Herman Teppis, Collie Munshin, the Congressional investigating committee), he came to interest Mailer rather more in the nuances of his affair with Elena. Gradually Mailer came to place this affair at the center of his book, using the other characters and episodes to define its significance. Eitel's affair with Elena is not, as Richard Chase has suggested, "a small masterly novel within a novel";[6] it *is* the novel, at least its central movement.

Few critics have been moved to speak of a central movement in their readings of *The Deer Park*. It has been assumed that Mailer used the book to indulge a variety of his personal interests: the precarious position of the artist in America, Hollywood, the sexual revolution, the advent of the hipster, etc. It has been assumed that he divided his narrative interest more or less equally among three characters, Sergius, Eitel, and Marion Faye. It has been assumed, in other words, that *The Deer Park* has no center, no structural or thematic unity. The novel has been respected—*when* it has been respected—for its local successes, its successful parts: its humor, its satire on the movie world, at times its delineation of the Eitel-Elena love affair. What Chase says about this affair is really quite typical, for he assumes that in a novel so loosely organized this episode must be considered apart from its context in Mailer's narrative.

My own view is that *The Deer Park* is a work of much greater unity than anyone has yet acknowledged. The novel is only incidentally a satire on Hollywood or an outlet for Mailer's philosophical predilections; at heart it is the story of a rather tragic love affair. In dealing with the book's minor and major characters, I hope to show that Mailer has used both his fictional world and his several subplots to enrich the central action of Eitel's "bad affair." I would also suggest that in the gaudy and seemingly unique mores of Hollywood Mailer has discovered the materials for his most impressive critique of postwar America.

I   *Desert D'Or: "that gorge of innocence and virtue"*

It is easy to see why *The Deer Park* has been taken as a formal satire.
Its fictional world of Desert D'Or (Palm Springs) is a satirist's delight.
It is a world marked by the varieties of sexual experience—a world of
"sandwiches" and "balls" (111),[7] multiple infidelities, even sexual
intercourse in telephone booths (238). It is a world whose hero is
glorified by rumors that he is an alcoholic, a drug addict, and a satyr
(28); a world whose most admirable figures are "a girl who's been
around" (186) and a professional pimp. Small wonder that Mailer has
been credited with detailing the lower regions of hell.[8]

This is not really Mailer's intention, however. His point is that the
excesses of Hollywood only mirror our common tendencies.
Moreover, what we share with Hollywood is something quite
different from its apparent "liberation." In the passage which follows,
Mailer is discussing contemporary America (circa 1959), but notice
how well he describes the world of *The Deer Park*:

> We have grown up in a world more in decay than the worst of the Roman
> Empire, a cowardly world chasing after a good time (of which last one can
> approve) but chasing it without the courage to pay the hard price of full
> consciousness, and so losing pleasure in pips and squeaks of anxiety. We want
> the heats of the orgy and not its murder, the warmth of pleasure without the
> grip of pain, and therefore the future threatens a nightmare . . . We've cut a
> corner, tried to cheat the heart of life, tried not to face our uneasy sense that
> pleasure comes best to those who are brave . . . (*Adv*, 23).

Just so, the world of *The Deer Park* is one in which everyone pursues a
good time while looking about furtively for the cops. What Mailer
remarks about Desert D'Or is not so much its immorality as its
profound sentimentality. The people of Desert D'Or *think* in terms
of traditional American values, whatever they may actually *do*.[9]

Desert D'Or betrays this discrepancy everywhere. This "all new"
society (1) is committed to "love" yet unable to avoid the most vulgar
commingling of love and lucre, sex and commercialism. Its "art" is
well represented by the sentimental movies Collie Munshin would
make from Eitel's screenplay and Sergius' life (178–80, 192–93). And
while apparently free of traditional moral restraints, Desert D'Or is
not free of a sentimental conformity. This is best seen in its respect for
the Congressional committee investigating "subversives" and Teppis' opinion that we should all *love* society (270). Desert D'Or's

respect for the committee is consistent with its pathetic efforts to keep up appearances—witness its love for publicity shots, proof positive of Teppis' claim that his studio, Supreme Pictures, is "a big family" (90); its obsession with achieving "decent healthy mature relationship[s]" (58); its willingness to abandon men like Eitel who stand for a time against "the public and professional voices of our sentimental land" (374). Mailer's distaste for this world is implicit in the novel's epigraph, a courtier's description of the pleasure court at Versailles: ". . . the Deer Park, that gorge of innocence and virtue in which were engulfed so many victims who when they returned to society brought with them depravity, debauchery and all the vices they naturally acquired from the infamous officials of such a place."

Mailer's attitude toward his fictional world is most evident in his portraits of Collie Munshin and Herman Teppis, two of Desert D'Or's more infamous officials. Munshin must be credited with the phrase Norman Podhoretz cites as most typical of Desert D'Or's hypocrisy. In conversation with Eitel and Sergius, Munshin suggests that what Elena really wants is "a decent healthy mature relationship" (58).[10] Munshin is also given to protesting that he is "a good liberal" (57, 181), though his liberalism, like his respect for "mature" relationships, is not much in evidence in the novel. In his operations as a Hollywood producer, Munshin in fact bears some resemblance to the notorious Sammy Glick.[11] His father-in-law, Herman Teppis, embodies even more impressively the division in Desert D'Or between public image and private fact. Publicly, Teppis has a most cheerful respect for traditional values. " 'I don't know people who feel respect for society any more,' " he laments. " 'In my day a man got married, and he could be fortunate in his selection, or he could have bad luck, but he was married' " (64). Teppis has "a large warm heart" for everyone (265), but especially for society: " 'I love society. I respect it' " (270). But even Teppis knows this simple piety is a fraud. Immediately after forcing one of his stock girls to engage in fellatio, Teppis murmurs, " 'There's a monster in the human heart' " (285). Certainly there is a monster in Teppis' heart in his dealings as a Hollywood mogul. The trappings of his office testify to that "large warm heart" he claims for himself: ". . . a famous painting of a mother and child was set in a heavy gold frame, and two hand-worked silver cadres showed photos of Teppis' wife and of his mother, the last hand-colored so that her silver hair was bright as a corona" (263–64). But it is beneath these pictures that Teppis carries on his campaign to marry Lulu Meyers to a homosexual actor for the publicity values involved (263–85). Like Munshin, Teppis embodies the schizophrenic blend of the sentimental and the amoral which is at the heart of Desert D'Or.

Mailer's critique of his fictional world is important because it is *America* that he confronts in *The Deer Park,* not just an exotic, atypical community of Hollywood stars, starlets, and executives. In the machinations of Munshin and Teppis, Mailer catches Hollywood in the act of producing what he has elsewhere described as "the sentimental cheats of the movie screen" (*Adv*, 23). But the typical Hollywood movie resembles Mailer's America. It pursues pleasure "without the courage to pay the hard price of full consciousness"; it tries "to cheat the heart of life"; it evades what Sergius calls the "real world . . . a world of wars and boxing clubs and children's homes on back streets . . . a world where orphans burned orphans" (47). It evades, in short, the reality of evil; it suggests that we can get what we want at no real cost to ourselves. This sentimental faith is what America shares with Hollywood. In Munshin, Teppis, and the other "prospectors for pleasure" (4) of Desert D'Or, Mailer gives us the apostles of this tender creed.

It is also important that we see how this portrait of Desert D'Or functions in the novel as a whole. Mailer has not rendered the moral vagaries of Desert D'Or merely for purposes of satire. Like Fitzgerald in *The Great Gatsby* and Hemingway in *The Sun Also Rises,* Mailer has used his fictional world to define both the state of modern life and the moral status of his main characters. Just as we respect Gatsby's vision and Jake Barnes' courage in part because of the visionless and self-pitying people who surround them, so we appreciate Mailer's central figures—Eitel and Elena, Sergius and Marion—because of the contrast they make with their environment. Mailer's detailed creation of this world also establishes the moral context in which Eitel and Elena must act. Mailer's hero and heroine command respect because they try to get beyond their social world and its sentimental cheats; they would reject the accommodations of others for the risks and commitment necessary to growth. But if the commercialism, sentimentality, and hypocrisy of Desert D'Or make a vivid picture of what Eitel and Elena try to rise above, they are also the temptations to which Eitel especially falls prey. The value we place on this affair and the ultimate grounds for its failure cannot be understood apart from the context of Mailer's fictional world.

II   *Sergius and Marion*

The subplots involving Sergius and Marion have usually been seen as much less functional. Sergius is often discussed as the rather undistinguished hero of *The Deer Park,* and Marion has been called "a dark and unassimilated presence" in the book.[12] But their stories should not be judged as independent lines of action. They are of value insofar as they comment on the fate of Charley Eitel, the novel's true protagonist.

It is especially important that we understand the limited role assigned to Sergius, for if we isolate his story we are likely to be rather dissatisfied with it. Like Mikey Lovett in *Barbary Shore,* Sergius is the rootless narrator of his own story. Brought up in an orphanage, he has "no place to go, no family to visit" after he is discharged from the Air Force at the beginning of the novel. He goes to Desert D'Or in search of "a good time" (1), but his quest has more to do with identity than with pleasure. What Sergius lacks is a solid sense of self. In his first months at Desert D'Or he admits to feeling like an unemployed actor (5), an impersonator (19), a spy and a fake (21, 46). His experience of the world is that of an alien: "I was never sure of myself, I never felt as if I came from any particular place, or that I was like other people" (21). Only once has Sergius found a temporary refuge from this feeling—during his experience as a bomber in Korea—but "that home fell apart" (45) when he discovered the consequences of his bombing missions. His experiences in Desert D'Or are no happier. Like Augie March, he comes to feel that he must look elsewhere for a fate good enough; he must, it seems, renew his quest in the bull rings of Mexico and the lofts of Greenwich Village (349-54).

But what is Sergius looking for? Even as the novel ends, he cannot really tell us: ". . . do we not gamble our way to the heart of the mystery against all the power of good manners, good morals, the fear of germs, and the sense of sin? Not to mention the prisons of pain, the wading pools of pleasure, and the public and professional voices of our sentimental land. If there is a God, and sometimes I believe there is one, I'm sure He says, 'Go on, my boy. I don't know that I can help you, but we wouldn't want all *those* people to tell you what to do' " (374). By the end Sergius has evaded the sense of sin and the wading pools of pleasure; he has stopped listening to the public and professional voices of our sentimental land. But if he has arrived at the heart of the mystery, he doesn't reveal its secret to the reader. Mailer has told us that Sergius was "the frozen germ of some new theme" (*Adv*, 236). This theme would be Mailer's "American existentialism," his belief that we must create our own identities in a world we *always* make. Alas, it is a theme still frozen in the figure of Sergius. Mailer has dramatized enough of his encounter with Desert D'Or and its "infamous officials" to justify Sergius' retreat from the resort and subsequent search for a different life style, but he has hardly prepared us to accept Sergius' bullfighting and his bullfighting school as forays into "the heart of the mystery." Mailer has argued that for the existentialist "a life which is directed by one's faith in the necessity of action is a life committed to the notion that the substratum of existence is the search, the end meaningful but mysterious" (*Adv*, 341). Presumably we are to see Sergius as carrying on this search from the bull rings of Mexico to his loft in the Village, but this whole final episode lacks conviction.

This shouldn't be the final word on Sergius, however. Mailer never intended that we should take Sergius as the novel's hero, nor that we should read his story apart from Eitel's. In his essay on *The Deer Park*, Mailer refers to the offer Sergius receives of a movie career and the consequences of his refusal—his separation from Lulu Meyers and withdrawal from Desert D'Or. Mailer remarks that this entire episode "had never been an important part of the book" (*Adv*, 243). As I have suggested, the *important* part of the book concerns Eitel and Elena. What we have of Sergius is more than enough to clarify his relationship to Eitel—and this, finally, is what matters.

Sergius comes to Desert D'Or in search of a viable self; in Charley Eitel, he finds a model. At first Sergius is very much the innocent, Eitel the wise instructor. When Eitel says that his Rumanian mistress was "passionate in a depressing way," Sergius demands of him, " 'How can passion be depressing?' " (35); later, he sees nothing ridiculous in his hope that Lulu will "give up the movies" (229). Sergius understands neither himself nor the world; in Mailer's terminology, he doesn't know how things work.[13] Through his friendship with the older Eitel, however, he quickly learns some of the necessary discriminations. Early in the novel he is an uncritical member of Dorothea O'Faye's notorious "court," but after meeting Eitel he finds that "Dorothea's charm had turned, and the better I came to know her the less I was impressed by her" (139-40). Sergius also comes to reveal a more critical attitude toward such hangers-on as Jay-Jay (140-41) and real insight into the complexities of Marion

Faye (147). He becomes progressively more reliable as a guide to the moral climate of Desert D'Or.

Ironically, this is most important as it relates to Sergius' changing views on Eitel. Precisely because Sergius becomes more reliable, his doubts about Eitel become the reader's own doubts. Sergius first sees Eitel as a victim of that "real world" he had discovered in Korea: "I had the notion that there were few kind and honest men in the world, and the world always took care to put them down. For most of the time I knew Eitel, I suppose I saw him in this way" (23). Sergius both identifies with and idealizes Eitel: "I felt that he was a man like me, only many times smoother and he knew more" (29). Later, commenting on what he has learned in Desert D'Or, Sergius will say, "Eitel is very different from me" (100). Between these last two statements we have Sergius' development in *The Deer Park*. What Sergius comes to see is that Eitel is as much at fault as the "world"—precisely the point Mailer has made concerning the tragedy of Eitel and Elena (*Adv*, 238). When Sergius finally turns on Eitel, his judgment may lack something in compassion, but it does not lack authority (302-08).

Mailer builds this judgment into the very structure of his book, for he has chosen to counterpoint Sergius' growth and Eitel's moral decline. At the beginning of the novel each man is recovering from the most devastating experience of his life—for Sergius, the breakdown which follows his recognition of the "real world"; for Eitel, the loss of his career because of his stand against the investigating committee. Each is afflicted with impotence (both literal and figurative). During the novel the two men undergo similar experiences. Each enters into a love affair which resolves the immediate problem of impotence but leads to a more serious moral dilemma; each is tempted by the commercialism of Hollywood (commonly represented by Munshin and Teppis); each is forced to decide whether or not he was meant to be an artist. The two stories make an ironic contrast. As Sergius detaches himself from Lulu Meyers, rejects the temptation of Hollywood, and dedicates himself to becoming a writer, Eitel fails in his affair with Elena, gives in to Munshin and Teppis, and admits to himself that he is not an artist. As Sergius grows, Eitel declines. Sergius is therefore of great value to Mailer in defining the more central action of Eitel's moral failure. Mailer's rather vague treatment of Sergius at the end of the novel is unfortunate, but it would be a major flaw only if the book had focused on Sergius' "education." As the novel stands, it is enough that we last see Sergius still in search of a better life, no longer "one of those boys for whom losing came naturally" (20). For this tends to highlight Eitel's too graceful acceptance of defeat before the public and professional voices in America and in himself.

Mailer's existentialist leanings are also relevant to his treatment of Marion Faye. Marion anticipates Mailer's interest in the hipster, the true American existentialist. In "The White Negro" (1957), Mailer argues that the hipster is a product of this century's countless atrocities, especially the invention and use of the atomic bomb. Because we have been forced to live with death as a constant possiblility, the honest response to our condition is "to accept the terms of death, to live with death as immediate danger, to divorce oneself from society, to exist without roots, to set out on that uncharted journey into the rebellious imperatives of the self" (*Adv*, 339). Mailer sees the hipster as engaged in just such a journey. The hipster's faith is good existentialist doctrine: one must divorce oneself from society and shape reality to the form of one's needs; the rebellious imperatives of the self must be obeyed or one will go under, for "life is a contest between people in which the victor generally recuperates quickly and the loser takes long to mend" (*Adv*, 349). Life is a war and help must come from within or not at all. As Mailer says, "The unstated essence of Hip, its psychopathic brilliance, quivers with the knowledge that new kinds of victories increase one's power for new kinds of perception; and defeats, the wrong kind of defeats, attack the body and imprison one's energy until one is jailed in the prison air of other people's habits, other people's defeats, boredom, quiet desperation, and muted icy self-destroying rage" (*Adv*, 339). Which is not a bad account of what happens in *The Deer Park* to Sergius (the "victor"), to Eitel (the "defeated"), and to Marion himself.

Marion has seemed to many readers to be the hipster incarnate. Mailer remarks of hipsters that while they are few in number "their importance is that they are an elite with the potential ruthlessness of an elite." Marion is nothing if not an elitist with a potential—nay, a kinetic—ruthlessness. Mailer distinguishes the hipster from the pure psychopath by the hipster's "absorption in the recessive nuances of one's own motive which is so alien to the unreasoning drive of the psychopath." Again, Marion's self-scrutiny is almost obsessive. Further, Mailer describes in "The White Negro" both the *ideal* hipster and the *actual* hipster as of 1957. In the passage which follows he speaks of the psychopath where he means to define the hipster (a "philosophical psychopath"—*Adv*, 343) as he exists at present:

At bottom, the drama of the psychopath is that he seeks love. Not love as the search for a mate, but love as the search for an orgasm more apocalyptic than the one which preceded it. Orgasm is his therapy—he knows at the seed of his being that good orgasm opens his possibilities and bad orgasm imprisons him. But in this search, the psychopath becomes an embodiment of the extreme contradictions of the society which formed his character, and the apocalyptic orgasm often remains as remote as the Holy Grail, for there are clusters and nests and ambushes of violence in his own necessities and in the imperatives and retaliations of the men and women among whom he lives his life, so that even as he drains his hatred in one act or another, so the conditions of his life create it anew in him until the drama of his movements bears a sardonic resemblance to the frog who climbed a few feet in the well only to drop back again (*Adv*, 347).

Marion is much like the frog. Repeatedly he tries to purge his "compassion" and cleanse himself of what he calls the world's "bullshit," to forge his own character despite "the conditions of his life." Marion is this kind of hipster—a *failed* hipster.

But even this is misleading. Mailer suggests that both the ideal and actual hipster are searching for the "apocalyptic orgasm"—not Marion's style at all. Mailer speaks of "the hipster, rebel cell in our social body, [who] lives out, acts out, follows the close call of his instinct as far as he dares" (*Adv*, 363); he approves the hipster's emphasis on "the need of his body" (*Adv*, 341); he defines Hip as "the affirmation of the barbarian" (*Adv*, 355). Instinct, body, barbarian—these terms are not easily associated with Marion Faye. Marion is profoundly distrustful of his instincts: "He could be impregnable if sex was of disinterest to him and that was how to be superior to everybody else" (156). In fact, Marion is the hipster's opposite number, always acting from reason, never from instinct. When his rational decisions fail because his emotions intrude, Marion feels "defeated" instead of liberated (341). Marion is a much more complex figure than the programmatic hipster of Mailer's essay. All he really shares with this romantic figure is a sense of *mission*. The end of his search is, like that of Mailer's hipster, "meaningful but mysterious." Mailer might have been thinking of Marion when he came to write of the hipster's "goals": "What is to be created is not nearly so important as the hipster's belief that when he really makes it, he will be able to turn his hand to anything, even to self-discipline" (*Adv*, 351). Marion's "black heroic safari" (328) is such a quest for greater self-control. Neither he nor his creator can be more specific.

It follows that Marion's values are exclusively negative— repeatedly we are told what he does *not* like. The essence of his thought is that "the whole world is bullshit" (17). "Bullshit" is shorthand for the fabulous illusions we live by, the values we read into our acts. Such an illusion is man's faith in love, and Marion has his remedies for such pretension: "No one ever loved anyone except for the rare bird, and the rare bird loved an idea or an idiot child. What people could have instead was honesty, and he would give them honesty, he would stuff it down their throats" (155). As Sergius notices, Marion is an inverted saint whose message is the vileness of human nature and whose single consolation is the honest acceptance of one's corruption. It is this perverse integrity which makes Marion so useful to Mailer, for Marion's role is to comment on and influence the novel's action. The book's "evil genius,"[14] Marion stands apart from the other characters and casts a very cold eye on their inconsistencies and vices.

Marion is most often employed as Eitel's conscience. As such, he is crucially involved in several of Eitel's more important decisions. It is Marion who reinforces Eitel's desire to resist the subversive commit- tee, arguing that to capitulate would merely allow Eitel to go on making commercial motion pictures: " 'You'll just keep cooking slop till you die' " (41). Later, it is Marion who tempts Eitel with the possibility of being unfaithful to Elena (186-87). These two episodes mark respectively the high point in Eitel's moral history and the end of his struggle to make it with Elena. In each case Marion encourages an action which will epitomize Eitel's moral condition of the moment. He is also crucial to the aftermath of the second episode, Eitel's liaison with the callgirl, Bobby. When he demands that Bobby pay him $167 of the $500 Eitel has given her, Marion helps define our complex response to Eitel's gesture. Marion's demand points up Eitel's sentimental weakness in giving Bobby so much money, while it also creates sympathy for Eitel's more compassionate treatment of the girl. The grounds for Eitel's tragedy are implicit here, for Eitel is both weak *and* compassionate.

Marion also helps shape our views on Elena. He first sees Elena as potentially one of his "girls": " 'Charley, you know like I know, she's just a girl who's been around' " (186). Marion tries to think of Elena as he thinks of Bobby: as someone who must have honesty stuffed down her throat. He has considered instructing Bobby in her own nature by humiliating her sexually, but for Elena he has greater plans. He senses the profound loneliness in Elena; he thinks that her nature is suicidal and that she must be taught this truth about herself: she must be made to commit suicide. But Marion can't rid himself of "a pure lump of painful compassion" for Elena (334)—she is more than a girl who's been around, and he cannot deny this greater depth in her. Of particular relevance is Marion's opinion of Elena when he thinks she is dead: " 'She was better than the others,' he said to himself. 'She was the strongest of the whole lot' " (340). It is a sign of the times that Mailer should use Marion Faye as a reliable commentator, but such is the case. Marion's last words on Elena measure her ultimate stature in the novel.

Marion's own story is concluded in these final pages. This is the story of his unhappy love affair with an idea. Marion's "idea" follows from his belief that the world is "bullshit." Everything is phony; the world's advice is worthless; to listen to the world is to invite what Marion hates most in life—slavery (15). And "slavery" is anything which restricts freedom of the will: ethical prescriptions, the demands of a business, even compassion ("Compassion was the queen to guilt"—p. 160). Marion's "idea" is that life must be dominated through a merciless exercise of reason and will. Our emotions are taught us by the world and the world is a whore.

Marion's nihilism makes him an excellent witness against the hypocrisies of others, but it is not an easy philosophy to live by. This is especially true for Marion, who is by nature sensitive, even tender. Marion must *teach* himself to resist his emotions. Because he feels fear at night, he must leave his house unlocked (150-51). Because he is afraid he will attach a sentimental value to sex, he must become a pimp. Because he "burns" for Paco, a poor Mexican in need of a fix, he must refuse the boy money—he must beat off compassion or play the victim to his emotions (160). Such a program for stifling one's feelings must end in failure. Though he rejects the mystique of sex by becoming a pimp, Marion ends up "in trade," a common businessman—an exchange of one "prison" for another (328). His efforts to make Elena kill herself are a conscious attempt to break out of this prison and give his life a diabolic "purpose," but he cannot follow through: ". . . he had his drop of mercy after all" (341).

From our point of view, Marion's "defeat" is his victory. His story is a thematic inversion of Eitel's, for while Eitel struggles to live up to his feelings for Elena, Marion struggles to rid himself of his emotions altogether. Both men "fail," but their failures mark very different endings. We must take Eitel as we find him at the end of the novel, for he has lost the desire to *search*. It is different with Marion. We last see Marion on his way to a real prison, but his final words are not those of a defeated man: " 'I have the feeling I'm just getting on to it' " (347). Perhaps Marion has begun a search less self-defeating than his quest for an omnipotent will. We cannot be sure, no more than we can be sure that Sergius will discover the "meaningful but mysterious" end to *his* search. But this very uncertainty is what deepens our sense of Eitel's contrasting, irreversible commitment to the coward in himself who has chosen the easy route of prestigious mediocrity. In his last appearance, as throughout the novel, Marion thus contributes to our understanding of Eitel.

III   *Eitel and Elena*

If Mailer has skillfully integrated his fictional world and his several subplots into the action of *The Deer Park*, his most impressive achievement is still his treatment of Eitel and Elena. I would agree with Richard Foster that "as we move toward the core of this book—the affair between Elena and Eitel—surely we move from the impressive into the field of force of something like 'greatness.' "[15] Whatever its other virtues (and vices), *The Deer Park* is strongest at its center.

As the novel is about the moral defeat of its hero, Charles Francis Eitel, it should be helpful to summarize Eitel's career prior to the represented action. Mailer provides such a summary early in the book, where he reveals that Eitel is typical of that generation of Americans born into the Depression. The son of immigrant parents, "first of his family to go to college" (30), Eitel has married young and pursued his own interest (the theater) as well as his wife's (radical politics). His work in the New York theater has brought him a reputation as a promising director and finally a call from Hollywood. There he has managed to make three low budget films which are still valued as realistic masterpieces. In the years which follow, Eitel has involved himself in the Spanish Civil War (a final gesture of "commitment" to the left); returned to Hollywood and shed his wife (he will go through two more divorces); and achieved, in fifteen years and twenty-eight pictures, a huge commercial success largely based on technical virtuosity rather than art. Like many men of "humble beginnings," Eitel has worked very hard to achieve a dubious celebrity. Once dedicated to the art of the theater, he has come to realize that "he would always be making the studio's pictures . . . his true marriage was with the capital" (36).

When we first meet him, of course, Eitel is making no pictures at all. After years of compromising his integrity, Eitel has lost everything as a result of one principled action: his refusal to cooperate with the Congressional investigating committee. This admirable gesture has led to his being blacklisted in Hollywood. We first see Eitel during his exile in Desert D'Or, where he is working on a new film script which he views as "another chance" (44), an art work which will redeem his years in Hollywood. This work has gone very badly, for Eitel has discovered that he cannot function without the nourishment of Hollywood's fortune and esteem. A fabled lover, Eitel has been reduced to impotence by his forced withdrawal from the protective atmosphere of Hollywood. He is plagued by self-doubt and a fear that he has lost his capacities for art and pleasure alike; he has no answer for the voice in himself which admonishes that he cannot succeed without Hollywood.

It is at this point that Eitel meets Elena Esposito, Munshin's former mistress. Inspired by his ability to make love to Elena, Eitel recaptures his lost vitality and returns to his film script. In the long course of his novel, Mailer charts the consequences of this affair for Eitel's talent and character. Ultimately, however, we are less concerned with whether Eitel can be restored to achievement and self-esteem by a love affair than with the question of whether he can make it with Elena. It is Elena who represents "another chance" for Eitel, not his script.

This is to suggest that Mailer's basic subject is Eitel's love affair. Eitel's relationship to Hollywood, cited by Millgate and others as the book's focal point, is resolved before the novel is half over. Eitel capitulates to Munshin by page 178, where he admits to himself that his projected masterpiece is "impossible." The rest is detail: eventually he will arrange to work for Munshin and Teppis as he has always done. Surely we are not intended to see this decision as in any sense climactic. Rather, it is an important stage in the disintegration of Eitel's affair with Elena. It is the working out of this affair which occupies the rest of Mailer's novel.

If this isn't obvious, one reason is that Mailer also develops the affair between Sergius and Lulu Meyers. This second affair should be seen as a comic foil, however. There are many points of resemblance. Each affair begins with a marvelous first night which rids the man of his temporary impotence; each leads to an immediate rise in the man's self-esteem ("How I loved myself then," Sergius thinks after making love to Lulu—p. 96; "Loving himself, loving her body as it curled against him . . . [Eitel] fell asleep a happy man"—pp. 103-04); each goes from a first night extravaganza to a momentary, morning-after depression (104, 130); each costs the man great anguish when he is first separated from his beloved (113-15, 129-30). More generally, both affairs are as unpredictable as Lulu's moods, and much of our interest is in following the irrepressible ups and downs the two couples are always suffering. Mailer's use of counterpoint in this matter is quite deft. With their obvious parody of the All-American couple (both are blonde, blue-eyed, and beautiful), their games of seduction ("I was the photographer and she was the model; she was the movie star and I was the bellhop; she did the queen, I the slave"—p. 138), and Lulu's superb capriciousness and vanity, Sergius and Lulu tend to set off the very human anxieties and greater seriousness of Eitel and Elena. Indeed, Eitel and Elena play for higher stakes than do their younger counterparts. When *they* fail, it isn't an experience to assimilate and value. In Hemingway's phrase, it is truly the end of something.

Mailer develops this crucial affair with an almost Proustian sense for nuance. In this respect his treatment of Eitel and Elena is unique, for nowhere else in Mailer's fiction is a love relationship developed so fully. The passages devoted to Eitel and Elena are alternately amusing and pathetic, inspiriting and painful. Above all, they are human. They do complete justice to Mailer's distinction between fictional "characters" and "beings." Mailer has suggested that "a character is someone you can grasp as a whole, you can have a clear idea of him, but a being is someone whose nature keeps shifting."[16] Mailer offers Lulu as an example of the latter, but the real "beings" in *The Deer Park* are Eitel and Elena. This is especially true of Elena, Mailer's one successful feminine character. Like other American writers of the first rank, Mailer has had his troubles with the subject of sexual love, but *The Deer Park* shows that he is capable of treating the ambiguities of love with both respect and a fine sensitivity.

We may come to sympathize with Elena rather more than with Eitel, but the story Mailer tells is still basically Eitel's. What Mailer traces is Eitel's inability to redeem his past. What he dramatizes is Eitel's sentimental belief that the past can be redeemed without radical change of the self. Sergius remarks at one point that Eitel is "profoundly sentimental about sex" (110). Mailer is suggesting that

Eitel sees in sex a sufficient antidote to all the bad habits he has accumulated in Hollywood. He leaves no doubt that Eitel is critically sentimental about the power of sex to override the effects of the past. The evidence for this is the rest of *The Deer Park*. What are we shown if not the failure—the inevitable failure—of Eitel's most cherished and sentimental hopes?

It is Eitel's dream that "together each of them would make something of the other" (110). Together they will try to confirm Eitel's most secret conviction: "the core of [his] theory was that people had a buried nature—'the noble savage' he called it—which was changed and whipped and trained by everything in life until it was almost dead. Yet if people were lucky and if they were brave, sometimes they would find a mate with the same buried nature and that could make them happy and strong" (121). The last of the romantics, Eitel hopes to bring to the surface the buried nature in Elena and himself. Indeed, he hopes that their natures *are* common. But they are not common, as Eitel must finally acknowledge (257). There is in Elena the "noble savage" he postulates, but its equivalent in Eitel has been irreparably changed and whipped and trained by everything in life, the life he has chosen to live for too many years. Eitel's belief that his buried nature has been revivified by Elena is indeed profoundly sentimental—as if growth could come to him as a gift and not through his own acts.

This is not to say that Mailer lacks sympathy for Eitel and his romantic aspirations. If Eitel's dream is romantic, so is his creator. Mailer has said that "the sickness of our times for me has been just this damn thing that everything has been getting smaller and smaller and less and less important, that the romantic spirit has dried up, that there is almost no shame today like the terror before the romantic" (*Adv*, 382). In this spirit Mailer has proposed any number of "romantic" alternatives to our pragmatic and deadening social life (e.g., we should combat juvenile delinquency by holding "medieval jousting tournaments in Central Park"—*TPP*, 22; we should elect John F. Kennedy in order to restore "the dynamic myth of the Renaissance—that every man was potentially extraordinary"—*TPP*, 39). Mailer has also shown an exceptional—and romantic—concern for religious concepts such as salvation and damnation; not, it would seem, because he is religious in a conventional sense, but because such beliefs infuse life with meaning. Eitel shares this desire for the romantic, but he lacks Mailer's conviction that we must *earn* our romanticism. In Mailer's view, we pay for everything we get in life and to deny this is to entertain a profound sentimentality. As he says in the passage quoted earlier, "We want the heats of the orgy and not its murder, the warmth of pleasure without the grip of pain." It is so for Eitel, who must act in new ways and embrace new values if he is to have Elena but cannot do so.

Mailer portrays Eitel's failure in three stages. There is first the beginning of the affair, where Eitel imagines a future transfigured by the power of sex. In chapters fourteen through sixteen, however, Mailer dramatizes Eitel's reversion to old, old habits. At the start of chapter fourteen we see Eitel, depressed and disillusioned, six weeks into his affair. Before we return to follow Eitel's movements during these weeks, we learn that he has already been unfaithful to Elena. Mailer removes suspense while inviting us to follow the history of Eitel's failure. We are to concern ourselves not with the question of *whether* Eitel will fail but with *how* he has failed.

Eitel begins his affair with the conviction that he is insulated from the seductive pull of Hollywood, a notion he is quickly disabused of. First he is visited by a former assistant, Nelson Nevins. It develops that Nevins has inherited Eitel's women as well as the movies he used to make (165). Nevins inspires in Eitel "the pang of jealousy, call it more properly the envy he felt that he was being forgotten" (167). His visit prepares for the reappearance of Collie Munshin. Munshin has often worked with Eitel and hopes to do so again, despite Eitel's official status. Eitel must make a crucial decision at this point, for if he is to work for Munshin he must give up his conception of the script he is writing and accept Munshin's "improvements," all of them dishonest and sentimental but commercially viable (178-80). This decision is crucial because to accept Munshin's proposition is to abandon the desire to be an artist.

Eitel capitulates soon after he begins to meet with Munshin. He has had a terrible time writing his script about "a modern saint" who has risen to fame by exploiting the miseries of others on a television show, then sickening of his work has left the show to live amidst the poverty and suffering he has exploited to finally end his life a suicide (126-27). This script is at once a reworking of *Miss Lonelyhearts*[17] and a warning from Eitel to himself that he must not go back to his former life. Like the hero of his script, Eitel has been willing to "market sentiment and climb the heights of his own career" (126), all the while contemptuous of the audience he has fed with false and crippling emotion (assuming, as Eitel and Mailer do, that the artist has a measurable effect on his audience). Like his hero, Eitel must reject his "success" and begin anew. Unfortunately, he can imagine for neither his hero nor himself a life capable of embodying his newfound integrity. The suicide of his hero foreshadows Eitel's "selling" himself to Munshin (199).

Eitel thinks that his affair begins to fail because "the world had come" (164) in the form of Nevins and Munshin, enticing him with its comforts and prestige. But Nevins and Munshin are only catalysts who revive Eitel's longing for his old status. Indirectly, they bear the message that Elena must go, for Eitel believes that if he is to take up his former role in Hollywood he must do so without Elena. She has none of the talents she would need as the wife of a famous director. She is "timid with people" and "crude in her manners" (103); even "medium clever" conversation ruins an evening for her (172). By Hollywood's standards, Elena is a "fifth-rate woman" and Eitel a "second-rate man" (204). How would they ever manage together in Hollywood? This logic points to the more serious problem of Eitel's snobbery. It is he and not just Hollywood who thinks of Elena as a "fifth-rate woman." His dream is that together each of them would make something of the other, but it is *Elena* who must change. She is a "fishwife" (166) and "such poor material" for his remodeling program (167); "she was only what he could make of her" (115). Eitel can never forget that the two of them are, at the very least, highly dissimilar people. His arrogance is most evident in the conceit he invents while preparing Elena for the announcement that they must part: she becomes his "one hundred and fourteen pound sailfish" whom he must maneuver with "professional disinterest" (203). The columnist who remarks that Eitel is doing a "boudoir Pygmalion" with Elena is vulgar but not necessarily wrong (121).

Yet mixed with Eitel's arrogance is his profound guilt. Because Elena represents everything that Hollywood is not, Eitel is submerged in bad faith after submitting to Munshin and comes to desire "an affair with a woman for whom he cared nothing" (205). Eitel's disastrous liaison with Bobby climaxes the second stage of his affair. The events of the third and final stage are almost inevitable. Indeed, just as Mailer depicts Eitel *after* he has been unfaithful, then traces the steps which brought him to this act, so now he informs us that Eitel and Elena have separated *before* returning to narrate the final stages of their estrangement (290). As before, the effect is tragic. Simply by adjusting the chronology of his narrative, Mailer lends a sense of inevitability first to Eitel's indiscretion, then to his separation from Elena. Of necessity we are concerned with the process of their failure and how they respond to it, not the question of whether they will succeed or fail.

The last movement of Eitel's affair begins the night he attends one of Dorothea O'Faye's nightly parties. This party, as described in chapters eighteen and nineteen, inevitably recalls the party given by Teppis some months earlier. At that time Eitel and Elena took strength from their infatuation; Eitel retained sufficient courage to flaunt Elena before Teppis and his daughter, Lottie Munshin (91-93). Now Eitel and Elena are nearing the end of their relationship. Eitel spends most of the evening in conference with a congressman who has come to negotiate a second committee appearance for the suddenly "cooperative" Eitel (242-45). This submissive posture is repeated a few days later when Eitel and Elena participate in a "ball" at Don Beda's. Here Eitel's nerve collapses entirely, and he cannot forgive Elena for enjoying herself. He is utterly blind to Elena's stake in the experiment, the loneliness she momentarily escapes in the adoring eyes of Don Beda and his wife (293-94). Eitel has left Elena well before she leaves him to live with Marion.

Eitel is left with the comforts of rationalization: "What seemed most odious to him was that they had been tender to each other, they had forgiven one another, and yet he did not love her, she did not love him, no one ever loved anyone" (297). Eitel knows better. He knows that, in cold fact, "it was his own fault, finally it was always one's own fault" (164). Eitel has thought this much earlier, after his night with Bobby; but he is no less honest with himself now. He admits to Sergius that he has given in to Munshin because he wants his career with its attendant rewards: " 'You see,' Eitel was saying into my ear, 'it took me until now to realize I wanted such things very much, and that was why I stayed in the capital' " (226). He can tell himself that "if he had learned nothing else, he had learned that he was not an artist, and what was a commerical man without his trade?" (298). Eitel is even harder on himself in describing the messy details involved in retracting his testimony before the congressional committee: " 'So for the first time in my life I had the sensation of being a complete and total whore in the world . . .' " It is here that Eitel announces his one consolation: that he *knows* he is "disgusting" (306).

Later, Eitel will look back on these months in Desert D'Or as "the end of his overextended youth" (373)—as if he had salvaged maturity from his experiences of this period. The price has been high, however. He has not given himself to his affair with Elena; he has feared the changes he must make, the risks he must embrace. His reward is guilt and a timid repentance, for as Eitel realizes, "there was that law of life so cruel and so just which demanded that one must grow or else pay more for remaining the same" (346). Because he does not grow, Eitel must pay. Ironically, he must pay in part by marrying Elena. After her auto accident with Marion, Elena is helpless. She asks Eitel to marry her and he can only comply. Though he doesn't love Elena, he is responsible for her. Finally, Eitel is married to his past as well as to Hollywood. We last see Eitel in his sad "maturity," engaged in the professional routine of his career and an affair with Lulu Meyers. Always he must live with the knowledge that he and Elena have not made something of each other. Instead they have come to a compromise which allows Eitel to go his own way and strands Elena in "that domain where her problems were everyone's problems and there were no answers and no doctors, but only that high plateau where philosophy lives with depair" (372).

The conclusion of *The Deer Park* recalls Mailer's indebtedness to Hemingway. Mailer has said of Hemingway, "It is certain he created my generation—he told us to be brave in a bad world and to be ready to die alone" (*TPP*, 73). Mailer tells us something like this, too. As Robert Solotaroff has remarked, *The Deer Park* shows Mailer "clearly working his way toward the position that courage is the primary virtue."[18] This is Hemingway's lesson, of course: in a bad world (Desert D'Or, say), the one imperative is to have courage; to lack courage is to end as Eitel and Elena end. Yet Mailer's moral vision differs significantly from Hemingway's. Consider Frederic Henry's reflections at the end of *A Farewell to Arms*: "If people bring so much courage to this world the world has to kill them to break them, so of course it kills them. . . . It kills the very good and the very gentle and the very brave impartially." Henry's thoughts represent Hemingway's mature conviction that life itself is a tragedy.[19] Mailer would agree that to live in this world demands enormous moral stamina. But he would not blame our failures on the world alone. Throughout *The Deer Park*, in long passages of severe introspection, Mailer portrays Eitel's endless struggle with his conscience. He thus makes it clear that Eitel is not simply acted upon by the world of Desert D'Or or Hollywood. It is as Mailer has said: because Eitel and Elena "do more damage to one another than to the unjust world outside them," there is a hint of "the rare tenderness of tragedy" to their moral failure (*Adv*, 238). There is certainly a cruel sadness to it, emphasized by the fates of Sergius and Marion, who continue to struggle with the "unjust world" and so by contrast mark the complacency to which Eitel and Elena are reduced in the end.

This "rare tenderness of tragedy" applies more to Elena than to Eitel. Elena comes from the most depressing of backgrounds; as Eitel says, " 'My God, her parents brought her up with a meat cleaver' " (186). Once she leaves school her life is a series of affairs with men who only appreciate her talents in bed. She has no real chance to grow into the social role Eitel would demand of his wife; she is, all too painfully, a "social book-end" (86). Elena seems no more than what Marion first calls her, a girl who's been around. But she is much more than this, as first Eitel and then Marion discover. Eitel learns at once that outside the unfamiliar territory of "society," Elena is another person: "Never had he seen such a change. Where she was timid with people, she was bold with him; where crude in her manners, subtle with intuition" (103). This only convinces Eitel that Elena is an extraordinary lover. Later, he is to see the justice in Munshin's remark that Elena is "a person who hates everything that is small in herself" (57); he is to confirm what Sergius sees immediately: that Elena is "very proud" (81).

Elena's dignity is fully evident for Eitel (and for the reader) only with the letter she sends him following their separation (309-18). This letter is an ungrammatical but very perceptive analysis of their affair; repeatedly it captures the faults each of them has brought to the affair, and suggests, in its tone, an instinctive wisdom Elena has had too little opportunity to cultivate. It also reveals the terrible loneliness so evident in Elena's childish delight at being "the center of attention" with the Bedas (296) and perceived by Marion as the core of her character (327). Her loneliness has made Elena as fearful as Eitel; it has robbed her of the chance to act on her very decent insights. She has seen, for example, that both she and Eitel have wanted the other to solve all of life's problems: " . . . that's what you were asking me and what I was asking you and *I resented it as much as you did*" (315). Fearful of losing Eitel and being alone once again, Elena has remained silent and let this sickness grow until it is too late, Eitel's cowardice has asserted itself, and they have lost all chance of truly changing each other.

Elena's fear is so much more understandable than Eitel's, yet it too illustrates the theme which runs throughout *The Deer Park* and much of Mailer's later work. This is the theme describing contemporary America that Mailer formulated in a passage from *Advertisements for*

Myself (23) quoted earlier in this chapter as also fitting the world of this novel. The theme is not sex. Mailer's subject is rather our moral evasiveness. He offers his fictional world as an embodiment of this evasiveness, as the temptation Eitel and Elena must confront; he offers the stories of Sergius and Marion as alternative responses to this world and, therefore, as indirect comments on the more central and representative actions of Eitel and his mistress. Basically, however, Mailer dramatizes his theme in Eitel and Elena themselves. It is a prime virtue of this novel that in reading it we are aware only of their pathetic—perhaps tragic—plight. That their failure may also be America's only deepens the pathos and increases the tragedy.

CHAPTER 4

Mailer as Fabulist: The Novels of the 1960s

M OST of Mailer's fiction from 1948 (*The Naked and the Dead*) to 1955 (*The Deer Park*) can conveniently be termed traditional (or realistic). Only *Barbary Shore* (1951) represents a break with this fictional tradition and it is Mailer's one conspicuous early failure—a kind of Orwellian political novel which suffers from its author's attempt to develop both the complex personal relationships among its half-dozen major characters and their roles in a rather rigid allegory.[1] After 1955, however, Mailer seems to have reconsidered the premises on which his novels had been based, for a nine-year hiatus ensued in which no new novel appeared, and this silence was broken with such fictions as *An American Dream* (1965) and *Why Are We in Vietnam?* (1967). It seems generally agreed that these books represent a dramatic shift in Mailer's career as a novelist. In these novels, his critics inform us, Mailer abandons the realistic tradition which had nurtured his earlier works. But if Mailer's more recent novels mark a radical departure, what is the nature of this new direction? If Mailer gave up the realistic ghost when he serialized *An American Dream* in 1964, what other novelistic form did he embrace in doing so? These questions have seldom been asked, let alone answered, but I think they are essential to any genuine understanding of Mailer as novelist. *An American Dream* and *Why Are We in Vietnam?* have been applauded and deplored in the most extravagant terms, but it is hard to see how praise or condemnation can be meaningful unless we first grasp the formal nature of Mailer's recent experiments.

Of course, Mailer's critics usually feel no such reservation, for they are confident they do understand what Mailer was about in these books. Those who condemn the two novels are certain they are grotesque, unintentional parodies of the traditional novel; those who praise them are just as certain they replace that form with what we

like to call "the postmodern novel." My purpose in this chapter will
be to argue that in a real sense both positions are correct—and wrong.
Elements in these novels support either position and confirm
neither, for Mailer has indeed attempted something radical in his last
two novels. The results suggest, however, that he has failed to grasp
the full implications of his attempt. *An American Dream* and *Why Are
We in Vietnam?* are what I would call *formal* failures, for they
incorporate several fictional strategies without achieving the unity of
any single strategy. Their problems confirm Sheldon Sacks' argument
that a coherent fiction must be governed by a single synthesizing
principle, whatever the variety of its parts.[2] They also point to an
unfortunate marriage of theory and practice, for in both works Mailer
has fleshed out his own theories about the novel—theories which are
simply incommensurate with the possibilities of prose fiction. These
rather large claims must be clarified, of course, but first we must
examine the two novels in some detail.

I   An American Dream

In the January, 1964 issue of *Esquire*, Mailer's first novel in almost
ten years began to appear in serialized form. Eight installments later
it was finished, and in 1965 Mailer issued the book in a slightly
revised, hardcover edition. It was called *An American Dream*, and
none of Mailer's books had received quite the reception which
awaited this one. Granville Hicks wondered whether the book was "a
bad joke"; Philip Rahv argued that it lacked "verisimilitude, even in
the most literal sense"; Elizabeth Hardwick dismissed it as "a fantasy
of vengeful murder, callous copulations and an assortment of dull
cruelties."[3] Others were even more hostile, if that is possible.[4]
Any summary of the book's contents will quickly reveal what
offended its reviewers. *An American Dream* describes thirty-two
hours in the life of its hero, Stephen Richards Rojack, ex-war hero,
ex-Congressman, presently employed as a university professor
whose works expound "the not inconsiderable thesis that magic,
dread, and the perception of death were the roots of motivation" (8).[5]
At the beginning of the novel Rojack is suffering the pains of
estrangement from his wife, Deborah, but more generally he is
gripped by a sense of spiritual failure amidst the trappings of material
success. Before the first chapter is over, he has begun to remedy his
condition by murdering his wife. Much of the subsequent action
concerns his efforts to pass her death off as a suicide, but the police

interrogations are only a small portion of our hero's activities. He also makes love to two different women a total of four times; he falls in love with a blonde named Cherry, now involved with a gangster but formerly the mistress of Rojack's powerful father-in-law, Barney Oswald Kelly; he defends his right to Cherry by beating up her present lover, Shago Martin, a Black whom Rojack considers "the most talented singer in America" (181); he engages in a fierce, climactic confrontation with Kelly, who is associated not only with the criminal element in America but also with Satan himself; he suffers the loss of Cherry, who is killed by a friend of Shago's; and he resolves to go West, to Las Vegas. All of this, as the reviewers never tire of pointing out, in slightly more than a single day. Once he arrives in Las Vegas, Rojack has fantastic luck at the tables, wins enough to pay off his debts in New York, and decides to desert America. We last see him preparing to light out for the primitive wilds of Guatemala and Yucatan.

It is a commonplace that any plot summary will distort a writer's achievement, but the one offered above has the additional limitation of not suggesting all of the offending features in *An American Dream*. It should suggest why Rahv couldn't discover his cherished "verisimilitude," or why Hardwick would speak of "callous copulations." What the summary doesn't convey is the pervasive role of magic in the novel, those innumerable occasions where events are apparently determined by irrational "forces" rather than by human choices or chance, as if Rojack's "not inconsiderable thesis" about magic, dread, and the perception of death were Mailer's thesis as well. The novel does not so much describe Rojack's confrontations with the people in his life or such social representatives as the police, as it details his traffickings with white and black magic, the phases of the moon, and a host of instinctual "powers" which tell him what to do at all crucial moments and are associated quite seriously with God or the devil. For many readers, including the reviewers cited above, the ultimate vulgarity of Mailer's novel is its powerful suggestion that violence (including violent sex) is not an intolerable aberration but rather an extreme example of life's essential irrationality.

When his book first appeared, then, Mailer stood accused of violating both the canons of novelistic decorum and simple good sense. Since 1965, however, *An American Dream* has been defended by almost all of Mailer's serious critics. Indeed, it is often cited as the best of Mailer's novels, an opinion first advanced by the author himself.[6] Critics have explained the novel's oddities with one of three theories: that Mailer was writing a kind of Chaucerian or Dantean "dream-vision," not a realistic novel;[7] that Mailer was writing in the American tradition of romance rather than "the great tradition" of nineteenth-century English fiction;[8] that the book's extravagant events are the literary creations of its narrator-protagonist, not to be confused with the literal occurrences we expect in a novel.[9] All three theories share one basic assumption: to read *An American Dream* as a realistic novel is to misread it altogether. This sort of thinking has been so influential, I can think of no one who has questioned its plausibility since Leo Bersani offered the first counterattack on Mailer's reviewers, remarking, among other things, that "Mailer's latest novel has had the further distinction of provoking a quaint resurgence of neoclassical canons of taste."[10] Anyone who would question the persuasiveness of Mailer's novel must find himself aligned with the Rymers, Johnsons, and Popes of contemporary criticism. There are far worse things than espousing the standards of Samuel Johnson, but in any case I don't think the issue here is whether Mailer has a right to the kind of imaginative freedom a neoclassicist might find suspect. The issue is whether Mailer has in fact abandoned the conventions of realism, as his defenders so confidently assume.

It happens that Mailer has provided a number of comments on the formal nature of *An American Dream*: "When I wrote the novel, I had decided to take a pretty conventional movie story, or movie melodrama, and make it into a realistic novel";[11] "I wanted to write a novel of action, of suspense, of character, of manners against a violent background . . . *An American Dream* in a funny way becomes a novel of manners . . ."[12] Now, we are all familiar with the intentional fallacy and its pitfalls. Indeed, these quotations might illustrate the latter, for I am sure that Mailer's conception of a realistic novel is not Philip Rahv's or Elizabeth Hardwick's. Nonetheless, Mailer's remarks suggest that it is too easy to dismiss the illogical elements in *An American Dream* as romance conventions. We must face the possibility that in developing the details of his novel Mailer was, in Robert Solotaroff's phrase, "serious-serious."[13]

Mailer has offered another, more indirect commentary on *An American Dream*. Having learned that Hardwick's scathing review was to appear in *Partisan Review*, Mailer paid for "A Short Public Notice" in the same issue. In this two-page "reply" to Hardwick, Mailer reprinted a condensed version of John Aldridge's review of *An American Dream* which first appeared in *Life*. He remarks of

Aldridge's review, "I cannot pretend I was displeased to see it there [in *Life*], but I'm nearly as satisfied to see it here . . ."[14] Presumably, then, Mailer has put his stamp of approval on Aldridge's reading of the novel:

The novel explores, in what will surely be called morbid and salacious detail, the possibilities, not for damnation, but for salvation to be found in some of the most reprehensible acts known to our society—murder, suicide, incest, fornication and physical violence. It dramatizes the various ways a man may sin in order to be saved, consort with Satan in order to attain to God, become holy as well as whole by restoring the primitive psychic circuits that enable him to live in harmony with himself and find his courage, regardless of whether his courage seeks its test in the challenges of love or the temptation to murder, whether he ends by becoming saint or psychopath. It is, in short, a radically moral book about radically immoral subjects, a religious book that transcends the conventional limits of blasphemy to expose the struggle toward psychic redemption which is the daily warfare of our hidden outlaw selves.[15]

Perhaps the most interesting point about this passage is that Aldridge speaks of how Mailer's book "transcends" the conventional limits of blasphemy, not the conventional limits of the novel. This is important because it explains why Mailer could approve Aldridge's paraphrase and yet speak of the book as "realistic." The fact is that *An American Dream* was intended as *both* "a religious book that transcends the conventional limits of blasphemy" *and* "a novel of action, of suspense, of character, of manners against a violent background." Further, I think it can be shown that the book Mailer intended to write is also, for better or worse, the book he did write. *An American Dream* fails *because* of what Mailer tried to do, not because he failed to do it.

If we accept Aldridge's paraphrase, it seems clear that one thing Mailer tried to do was chart his hero's exemplary struggle toward spiritual health. As Aldridge says, Rojack sins in order to be saved, consorts with the devil in order to attain to God. His involvement with murder, sodomy, fornication, and other forms of physical violence is the necessary prelude to his "psychic redemption," for Mailer believes that only in successfully engaging our hidden outlaw selves can we revitalize a peculiarly American myth, "that each of us was born to be free, to wander, to have adventure and to grow on the waves of the violent, the perfumed, and the unexpected" (*TPP*, 39). Solotaroff has demonstrated that Rojack's story illustrates one of

Mailer's first principles: growth is possible only if we have the courage to confront our most violent possibilities, for true growth derives only from what Mailer likes to call "existential" situations, i.e., situations in which the outcome is both serious and uncertain.[16] Seen in this light, *An American Dream* is precisely what Solotaroff calls it: "a fictional rendering of Mailer's ontology."[17] And thus seen it becomes something like a Dantean dream-vision, as so many critics have argued.

On the other hand, the situation Mailer describes in *An American Dream* is not simply archetypal. This is, after all, an *American* dream, as almost all commentators acknowledge by citing as the *locus classicus* for discussion of the novel this passage from "Superman Comes to the Supermarket," an essay Mailer wrote in 1960:

> Since the First World War Americans have been leading a double life, and our history has moved on two rivers, one visible, the other underground; there has been the history of politics which is concrete, factual, practical and unbelievably dull if not for the consequences of the actions of some of these men; and there is a subterranean river of untapped, ferocious, lonely and romantic desires, that concentration of ecstasy and violence which is the dream life of the nation (*TPP*, 38).

This passage suggests that we should not see Rojack as Anyman working his way back to those primitive psychic circuits Mailer associates with God; rather, we should take him as a modern American, living in *the* modern city, New York, and suffering from the distinctly American schizophrenia summarized above. For Mailer, then, the "forces" which work on Rojack are both ontologically and socially real. In reading Mailer's one-volume encapsulation of the *Inferno, Purgatorio,* and *Paradiso,* we have no need for a fourfold critical analysis, nor even a twofold analysis, for the literal and the analogical are one.

This is the theory of it, at any rate. The practice is a good deal less persuasive, for uniting such diverse intentions leads to formal confusion, the frustration of any definite narrative expectations. In effect, Mailer has tried to combine the narrative forms Sheldon Sacks designates as "action" and "apologue." Sacks defines an action as "a work organized so that it introduces characters, about whose fates we are made to care, in unstable relationships which are then further complicated until the complication is finally resolved by the removal of the represented instability." Examples are *Tom Jones, Pride and*

Prejudice, and *Great Expectations.* An apologue is defined as "a work organized as a fictional example of the truth of a formulable statement or a series of such statements."[18] Examples are *Rasselas, Candide, Pilgrim's Progress,* and, indeed, *The Divine Comedy.* If I am right, *An American Dream* reads like a cross between *Great Expectations* and *Rasselas!* This suggestion might seem fanciful, but isn't it the case that Mailer's reviewers read his book as a contemporary *Great Expectations*—albeit a perverse version of Dickens' classic? And isn't it fair to say that Mailer's defenders have credited his novel with the form and moral seriousness, if not the moral stance, of Johnson's fable?

As I remarked earlier, these positions are both right and wrong, for each isolates certain features of the text while ignoring others. Like such traditional novels as *Great Expectations, An American Dream* employs realistic devices to create sympathy for its central character, to define the "instability" he must overcome, and to trace the course of events leading to removal of the instability. When Philip Rahv said that *An American Dream* was "written in the realistic convention,"[19] he was not merely imposing an alien tradition on the work of a "new" novelist. Rather, he was responding to Mailer's manifest desire to create believable, complex characters whose actions might seem extreme but not incredible. He was responding to scene after scene in which Rojack's psychological state and social situation are recorded with all the concern for "reality" we would expect of Jane Austen. In short, he was responding to those elements in the novel which explain Mailer's reference to the book as "a novel of manners." On the other hand, it is hard to credit Mailer's remark that "any intellectual aspects of *An American Dream* will have to be dredged up by the critics,"[20] for one critic, at least, has shown that nearly every episode illustrates Mailer's basic intellectual commitments, his "ontology." Solotaroff's brilliant discussion of the novel—essentially an elaboration of Aldridge's paraphrase—should persuade any reader that Mailer wanted to embody his philosophical/religious notions in the manner of Johnson, Voltaire, Bunyan, or Dante himself.[21] Whether he did so successfully is of course another question.

Indeed, it is a real question whether Mailer's novel succeeds as an action *or* as an apologue. As an action, *An American Dream* represents a slight modification of the form Sacks describes, for Mailer does not so much introduce characters in unstable relationships as he introduces *a* character in unstable relationship with himself. The "represented instability" is internal, not external, for Rojack is a man whose plight corresponds to Mailer's account of the way we live now: "Postulate a modern soul marooned in constipation, emptiness, boredom and a flat dull terror of death. . . . It is a deadening existence, afraid precisely of violence, cannibalism, loneliness, insanity, libidinousness, hell, perversion, and mess, because these are the states which must in some way be passed through, digested, transcended, if one is to make one's way back to life" (*TPP*, 283). Rojack is a man who must pass through these very "states," for in no other way can he achieve "a single identity at [his] center" (*CC*, 76). As an action, *An American Dream* is entirely concerned with describing this dark *rite de passage*, which perhaps explains why our sense of Rojack's inner life is immensely more vivid than that of the world around him, including the novel's other characters.

The first problem with the novel as action is that Mailer has done little more than "postulate" Rojack's desperate situation. It seems that his condition has something to do with his wife, especially the reasons he courted her; the manner in which he capitalized on his war record; his tendency to lecture about the motivating powers of magic and dread rather than to engage those powers directly in "real" life. We know all this because Rojack *tells* us about it in a five-page summary of his life just before he murders his wife. This summary is neither persuasive nor affecting, with the result that, in Sacks' terms, we don't come to *care* enough about Rojack. We identify with him to the degree that we identify with any first-person narrator, but we never feel the kind of sympathy a successful action requires. Certainly we don't feel the sympathy *this* protagonist requires when he plunges into acts of murder, sodomy, and psychic warfare. To create sufficient concern for such a hero, Mailer had to persuade us that Rojack's inner state was truly desperate, that he was on the verge of spiritual death at the hands of devilish social agents. But this would have required something like the hundreds of pages Dickens devotes to the social forces which have made Pip what he is.

The problem is that Mailer could not enter into such "novelistic" detail without detracting from the metaphysical implications of Rojack's rite of passage. Dante could introduce his hero's situation in a single stanza, remarking only that "Dante" had gone astray from the straight road and found himself in a dark wood, because the mode of Dante's great poem doesn't require that we care about its protagonist in a personal way. His fate concerns us only as it is exemplary, so the poet is well advised to ignore the specifics of his departure from the straight road. In trying to have it both ways, Mailer merely creates a murderer—scarcely acceptable as an exemplary figure even if the author might think him one—whose history is altogether too sketchy and enigmatic.

This failure to generate sufficient concern for Rojack is the novel's major problem as an action, but there are other difficulties. The most important of these is the nature of Rojack's quest for authenticity. Rojack submits to violence, insanity, libidinousness, perversion, *et al.* because he has come to believe "in grace and the lack of it, in the long finger of God and the swish of the Devil" (35). Such beliefs have led him to believe as well in following his instincts, his "inner voice." In this he merely practices what Mailer has often preached: "To learn from an inner voice the first time it speaks to us is a small bold existential act, for it depends upon following one's instinct which must derive, in no matter how distorted a fashion, from God" (*TPP*, 194). Rojack's inner voice tells him to kill Deborah, to approach Cherry, to remove Cherry's diaphragm during sexual intercourse, to fight Shago Martin, to confront Barney Kelly, to walk a parapet thirty floors over the sidewalks of New York City. Rojack listens and obeys in each case, so these events would seem the concrete stages in his quest for psychic redemption.

On the other hand, this inner voice and the actions it demands are also associated with the world of black magic and taboo, the world of the irrational. Rojack makes this association at one point: " 'God,' I wanted to pray, 'let me love that girl (Cherry), and become a father, and try to be a good man, and do some decent work. Yes, God,' I was close to begging, 'do not make me go back and back again to the charnel house of the moon' " (162). This desire to pull back from a perverse quest is not a momentary weakness on Rojack's part; it is repeated later when he argues with the inner voice that tells him to risk a dangerous journey to Harlem: "Let me love her some way not altogether deranged and doomed. It makes no sense to go to Harlem. Let me love her and be sensible as well" (208); it is repeated toward the end of the novel, when Rojack thinks, "I wanted to be free of magic, the tongue of the Devil, the dread of the Lord, I wanted to be some sort of rational man again" (255). What are we to think of Rojack's reservations about his quest? Indeed, what are we to think of the quest itself?

These questions lead to a more fundamental query: what kind of action does the novel present? Many readers have seen Rojack as a victim of neurotic—nay, psychotic—tendencies. These readers have sympathized with him at precisely those moments when he expresses the desire to be free of magic and its capricious demands. Can we be sure—from the text alone—that these readers are wrong? Can we share Aldridge's—and Mailer's—confidence that Rojack achieves salvation in the course of the novel, in which case his reservations are only momentary signs of weakness? The book offers only Rojack's point of view, as Mailer himself has reminded us,[22] and Rojack seems quite ambivalent on the issue. I think it is hard to avoid Stanley Gutman's suggestive conclusion: "The reader can never finally determine whether Rojack has, through magic, cut through rational conventions to a hidden significance, or whether he has entrenched himself more firmly in the illusory world of the psychotic."[23] Gutman doesn't seem to think this is an artistic problem, but I would suggest that it is a fatal, not an enriching, ambiguity. The story of a sick man who achieves health by cutting through rational conventions is a different story from that of a sick man entrenching himself more firmly in the illusory world of the psychotic. If we can never be sure which kind of story is unfolding, our response at all points must be quizzical, detached, essentially intellectual. The novel as action is crippled by such aesthetic distancing, for Rojack and his quest can never elicit the sort of emotional response Mailer presumably intended.

It would seem that Mailer expected us to read *An American Dream* with a close knowledge of his other works, especially his nonfiction, as an interpretive guide. Having written so often of that moral "plague" which invaded American life after World War II, Mailer presents his brief notations concerning Rojack's personal history as sufficient explanation for his hero's spiritual malaise. After all, doesn't Rojack suffer from all the tell-tale signs of that very plague? Having expressed his personal views in so many quarters, Mailer expects us to understand that Rojack is achieving authenticity when, for example, he interrupts the sexual act with Cherry to remove her diaphragm (127). After all, don't we all know how much our author detests contraception? But of course we don't all know this, nor should we be expected to. If *An American Dream* can't be understood without a working knowledge of *The Presidential Papers* (1963) and *Cannibals and Christians* (1966), volumes which collect Mailer's nonfiction of the early 1960s, no better explanation can be offered for the novel's failure as an action, for we can hardly be moved by characters and events which require an external gloss to be understood.

Much the same problem arises with the novel as apologue. Solotaroff has argued that *An American Dream* makes "fine sense as an exposition of ideas,"[24] but this is true only for those who are well versed in Mailer's private mythology. To make intellectual sense of the novel, we must again resort to Mailer's other works. The result is that Mailer's "formulable statement" is unacceptably private or obscure. This is true at almost any stage in the novel's "argument," but I think the point can be made by looking at two examples of Mailer's method.

Early in the novel Rojack tells of a war experience in which he saved his army company by killing four German soldiers. He explains that this action was made possible by "the clean presence of *it*, the grace" (5), an inspiration later defined as the sort of instinctual prompting Rojack must learn to trust at all times and not intermittently. Just before he killed the fourth German, however, Rojack made the mistake of looking into his victim's eyes, and in their presence he lost his "grace" and barely managed to kill the fourth soldier. Rojack says that these eyes "had come to see what was waiting on the other side, and they told me then that death was a creation more dangerous than life" (7). This experience continues to haunt Rojack in his subsequent career as a political, social, and academic lion in New York. Indeed, the message in these eyes is of major importance, for it precipitates the crisis which leads to the murder of Rojack's wife. It is fair to ask, then, what this "message" really amounts to.

The novel itself never answers this question, though it offers a belated hint or two. At the end Rojack sees such eyes again when he examines a cancer victim on an autopsy table (265-67). This is a strong clue for anyone who knows something of Mailer's theories about cancer. For Mailer, cancer results when the cells "betray" the body, when "they refuse to accept the will, the dignity, the desire, in short the *project* of the person who contains them" (*TPP*, 205). Cancer is a condition which comes to people who are dying spiritually, whose "projects" are inauthentic. What Rojack saw in the fourth German's eyes was a cancerous state. But how does this lead to the message that death is a creation more dangerous than life?

It leads to this idea via Mailer's notions about the human soul, death, and the possibility of a life after death. Mailer has affirmed the latter so many times, it is impossible not to take him at his word.[25] He believes "that we feel dread when intimations of our death inspire us with disproportionate terror, a horror not merely because we are going to die, but to the contrary because we are going to die badly and suffer some unendurable stricture of eternity" (*TPP*, 151). We die "badly" if we die in the state Mailer calls "cancerous"—the state of the fourth German soldier and the man on the autopsy table. Death is indeed a dangerous creation, for it might well involve the eternal loss of one's soul. It is this fear that Rojack reads in the German's eyes. It is this fear that comes upon Rojack himself when he refuses the moon's invitation to commit suicide in the novel's first chapter (11-13).

It is dangerous to dismiss this early episode as a fantasy, for the call of the moon is perilously close to those other irrational messages which appear everywhere in the novel. After not responding to this call, Rojack asks, "Will you understand me if I say that at that moment I felt the other illness come to me, that I knew then if it took twenty years or forty for my death, that if I died from a revolt of the cells, a growth against the design of my organs, that this was the moment it all began, this was the hour when the cells took their leap?" (13). What we are to understand is that this is the moment Rojack became cancerous ("a revolt of the cells"), and not, I fear, in any metaphoric sense. Behind Rojack's anxiety at this moment—the cause of his debilitating repression—is very much "a fear of dying," as Brom Weber has called it:[26] a fear "that death is not the end of anything, but is instead a continuation of the worst terrors of life" (*CC*, 363), the absolute worst being that the soul might "cease to exist in the continuum of nature" (*TPP*, 214).

Now, all of this is perfectly clear—to anyone who ponders Mailer's essays. I can't believe that anyone deprived of this guidance could understand the metaphysical implications of these early scenes. To the degree this is true, the novel as apologue must of course suffer. But then the novel also suffers when Mailer's implications are all too obvious, when his thought is relatively clear but insufficiently demonstrated, perhaps undemonstrable. The novel's climactic scene offers perhaps the best example of this. Throughout the book Rojack faces a series of moral and physical challenges, each requiring an extraordinary act of courage. This series culminates when he decides to walk the parapet on Barney Kelly's terrace. Rojack succeeds in negotiating the parapet once, but his "inner voice" warns him that the walk must be made *twice*—once for himself, once for Cherry. Because Kelly intervenes, Rojack doesn't make the second walk. The result? Rojack rushes back to Cherry's apartment and finds that she has been beaten to death.

Cherry's death cannot be seen as mere coincidence. The logic of the entire narrative argues that she dies because Rojack fails to traverse the parapet a second time. Rojack refuses to commit suicide when "instinct was telling [him] to die" (12), so the cells rebel and he becomes cancerous; Rojack and Cherry engage in authentic, loving sex (once that devilish diaphragm is removed), so Cherry conceives a child (176); Rojack does not "protect" Cherry by walking the parapet a second time, so she dies. The world of *An American Dream* is one in which such "magical" connections are stubbornly real. It is a world in which "good" (i.e., brave) actions are rewarded and "bad" (i.e., cowardly) actions are punished, a world in which poetic justice is writ very large. We can only conclude that one of Mailer's intellectual propositions goes something like this: acts of personal cowardice lead the powers that be to punish us by destroying what we value most. Such a conclusion is as hard to avoid as it is to accept.

The episodes involving the fourth German soldier and Cherry's death illustrate the novel's two problems as an apologue. The former betrays the fact that Mailer has neither developed nor clarified his rather complicated—and idiosyncratic—beliefs. (Indeed, it is hard to see how he could have done either, given the attention he must also devote to the novel's "realistic" elements.) An apologue is supposed to persuade us that certain propositions are true, but Mailer takes our assent for granted when he presents his ideas in such condensed, cryptic fashion. The inevitable result is obscurity. Conversely, the episode climaxed by Cherry's death suggests that Mailer has presented some ideas which cannot be dramatized convincingly. This may seem an arrogant opinion, but I doubt that the greatest artist could have presented the novel's climactic scenes so that their implications were persuasive.

Both of these problems are compounded by Mailer's insistence that the world of his novel is a "real" world.[27] Indeed, for Mailer it is *the* real world. This might explain his decision to mix the narrative modes of action and apologue, for in Mailer's view the world of his hero is our world as well. It seems not to have occurred to Mailer that the novelist has enough trouble persuading us that the world of his work is credible as either "real" or universally exemplary. Sacks has argued that the forms he defines as action and apologue are mutually exclusive, that a work of fiction cannot be organized coherently as part action, part apologue. Whether this is true of all novels needn't concern us here, but the example of *An American Dream* suggests that it is all too true of Mailer's fiction.

II   Why Are We in Vietnam?

Curiously, no one has remarked that Mailer's next novel, *Why Are We in Vietnam?*, suffers from the same formal problem as its predecessor. Even Solotaroff, the one critic who has questioned the "mixed modes" of *An American Dream*, argues that *Why Are We in Vietnam?* is entirely coherent and vastly superior as a novel. I would agree that *Why Are We in Vietnam?* is a much better novel, but I hardly think that it achieves "one constant, if complex, focus."[28] If anything, Mailer has mixed the modes of action and apologue even more radically here than in his previous work. The result is a brilliant but finally incoherent effort, the one Mailer novel which justifies the common complaint that his works succeed only in their parts, never as wholes.

The novel as action again focuses on its narrator-protagonist, in this case the eighteen-year-old Ranald Jethroe, or D. J. ("Disk Jockey to the world"). D. J.'s remarkably obscene narrative describes a hunting trip in Alaska when he was sixteen. The participants include D. J. himself; his best friend, Tex Hyde; his father, Rusty Jethroe; two of Rusty's subordinates at Central Consolidated Combined Chemical and Plastic, a Texas-based corporation; and Luke Fellinka, head guide for the Moe Henry and Obungekat Safari Group. The action centers, however, on D. J.'s relationship with his father, who is described by his son as "the cream of corporation corporateness" (29) and "the most competitive prick there is" (38).[29] This action includes three distinct stages, as D. J. first rejects his father and the upper middleclass culture he represents, then embraces the "new man" his father seems to become during the hunt, and finally rejects his father altogether once the change is revealed as illusory. These vacillations correspond to the early, middle, and late stages of the hunt itself, though this is often obscured by the onrushing scatological commentary of our young hero, a self-proclaimed "genius." For anyone who can discover the sensitive young man beneath the hip locutions and defiant brashness of D. J.'s rhetoric, the action is movingly developed. Its very simplicity, so unlike the exotic complexities of *An American Dream*, seems to revive Mailer's unique gifts for narrative.

These gifts are everywhere evident, especially in those set-pieces which describe the killing of a wolf (68-70), the tracking of a bear (135-41), the investigation of an arctic wilderness (173-204), or D. J.'s past and present experiences with his father (40-42, 127-34, 137-38).

Indeed, Mailer achieves some of the most oldfashioned effects associated with the novel as a form, for the *experience* of encountering a wilderness like the Alaskan Brooks Range filters through D. J.'s monologue with a force reminiscent of Conrad or Faulkner. In Conrad's sense, Mailer has made us *see* what the natural world is like in ways which compare with the best passages in *The Naked and the Dead*. In his portraits of Rusty, Rusty's flunkies, and the compromised old hunter, Luke Fellinka, Mailer has done much more than this, however. He has justified D. J.'s extreme alienation from his father's "civilized" world by rendering the careerism, hypocrisy, and vanity of these contemporary Americans, perhaps most tellingly in those scenes where the party uses helicopters to hunt wild game (98-105). Therefore we can sympathize with D. J.'s endless tirade against what he calls "implosion land," "this Electrox Edison world" (8), for its debilitating effects are seen everywhere in the novel's adult characters. We can, therefore, sympathize with D. J.'s efforts, late in the novel, to work himself free of "mixed shit" (184) by engaging the primitive world of Brooks Range without the "aid" of his father, such "guides" as Luke Fellinka, or even the tools of our technological age. We can feel the pathos of D. J.'s failure to succeed in this attempt signalled at the end by his decision to volunteer for active service in Vietnam because the forces of modern life which have made him what he is are so intractably strong.

The novel's virtues as an action could be described at much greater length, for they are real and impressive; but I fear it is more to the point to suggest how they are compromised by Mailer's insistence on burdening a tale of unhappy initiation with the materials of political and social allegory. The book's very title suggests that Mailer's aims are those of an apologue. The title hints that we are concerned here with "more" than the story of one boy's struggle with his family and culture. We are concerned with nothing less than an inquiry into the nature of contemporary America, specifically that sickness in the American character which has led to the infamous war in Vietnam. Unavoidably, then, we are encouraged to see the novel's events and characters as types. The artistic consequences are disastrous, for it is one thing to see a character like Rusty Jethroe as a certain kind of American personality but quite another to see him as America itself.

The allegorical elements in *Why Are We in Vietnam?* have often been cited, perhaps because they are so obvious. The chapter devoted to itemizing every piece of weaponry Rusty and his companions have brought with them to Alaska (77-90); those scenes depicting the use of helicopters to hunt wild animals; Rusty's story of the foul eagle, nature's most notorious scavenger (132-33)—these sections all too clearly represent, respectively, America's overwhelming material advantage over the Viet Cong, America's cowardly bombing tactics, and the scavenger-like nature of America's general enterprise in Vietnam. These scenes, and others like them, embody Mailer's intense hatred for our bullyish behavior in Vietnam, our obscene disregard for both nature and human life. The implications of such scenes are reinforced by D. J.'s commentary, which excoriates our amoral "Electrox Edison world" and suggests that the corporation types present on the Alaskan hunt are fully representative of the American character. The novel as apologue seems to insist that we are in Vietnam because, as Richard Poirier has put it, "we are as we corporately are."[30] What we are, in Mailer's paraphrase, is "a demented giant" suffering from "a fearful disease": "Greed. Vanity. . . . The Faustian necessity to amass all knowledge, to enslave nature."[31] What we are is sick.

The parabolic episodes cited above testify to this American sickness without offering a very precise diagnosis of its nature. They don't really tell us, in other words, why we are in Vietnam. Given Mailer's theory, however, it is perhaps unreasonable to expect a more specific analysis. Elsewhere Mailer has explored the same problem discursively, and his explanations have almost invariably been as general ("America is sick") as that proposed by his novel. In "A Speech at Berkeley on Vietnam Day," for example, Mailer offered this "explanation": "The great fear that lies upon America is not that Lyndon Johnson is privately close to insanity so much as that he is the expression of the near insanity of most of us, and his need for action is America's need for action; not brave action, but action; any kind of action; any move to get the motors going. A future death of the spirit lies close and heavy upon American life, a cancerous emptiness at the center which calls for a circus" (*CC*, 77-78). The next year, 1966, Mailer confirmed the drift of this analysis: "As is evident by now, the only explanation I can find for the war in Vietnam is that we are sinking into the swamps of a plague and the massacre of strange people seems to relieve this plague" (*CC*, 91). It was not until 1968 that Mailer came to suggest the nature of this "plague," which he defined as "a state of suppressed schizophrenia so deep that the foul brutalities of the war in Vietnam were the only temporary cure possible for the condition." He characterized this American schizophrenia as a devotion to the contradictory mythologies of Christianity and science ("The love of the Mystery of Christ . . . and the love of no Mystery whatsoever").[32] This idiosyncratic analysis really rests, of course, on Mailer's hatred for technology and its dehumanizing effects on any people who allow it to dominate their lives.

Mailer's entire canon testifies to his conviction that to embrace technology is to embrace as well "the Faustian necessity to amass all knowledge, to ensnare nature," so it is possible to square Mailer's paraphrase of the novel's meaning with his later, more analytical account of our motives in pursuing the war in Vietnam. What defies credibility is that we should be expected to see a man like Rusty Jethroe (or his underlings) as acting from a Faustian desire to amass all knowledge. Rusty and the others are, if anything, the mindless products of a system we might call Faustian, given Mailer's definition of the term; but as such they are effects, not causes. While it might seem presumptuous to ask that Mailer get at the *causes* of our American sickness, his own title generates this expectation. That his book doesn't satisfy such expectations perhaps explains why we sense something pretentious in Mailer's efforts to "expand" the significance of his work beyond the confines of D. J.'s personal story.

The novel as apologue suffers from other problems we have already seen in *An American Dream*. Once again Mailer has failed to fuse the events crucial to his hero's personal history and those crucial to his fictional argument (if such a merger is even possible); once again he has depended on our knowledge of his other works to understand the implications of his fable. Both problems can be illustrated by looking at one episode toward the end of the novel. When he turns away from the "mixed shit" of the hunting party, D. J. heads into the remoter wilds of the Brooks Range accompanied only by his friend, Tex Hyde. What ensues is an awe inspiring confrontation with perhaps the last of the American frontiers, climaxed by a night spent under the Aurora Borealis in which D. J. receives two messages: one, that "God was here, and He was real and no man was He, but a beast, some beast of a giant jaw and cavernous mouth with a full cave's breath and fangs, and secret call: come to me" (202), a God who admonishes, " 'Go out and kill—fulfill my will, go and kill' " (203); two, that D. J. should overcome his fears and engage Tex in homosexual relations (202). What are we to make of D. J.'s God, and what are we to think of D. J. when he fails to act on his desire for Tex? Presumably these are important and not peripheral questions, for they involve not only the climax of the hunting trip but of Mailer's novel as well.

D. J.'s "discovery" that God is a beast leads to his enlistment in

Vietnam, where he and his "killer brother" (204), Tex Hyde, can begin to satisfy this God's command to fulfill his will, go and kill. Knowing how Mailer feels about the war in Vietnam, several critics have assumed that D. J.'s God must be his own creation, the product of his enforced training in an overly competitive culture.[33] On the other hand, critics familiar with Mailer's other writings have identified this God with that instinctual "voice" both Rojack and D. J. must learn to trust.[34] If the first reading is true, Mailer is warning against the unchastened expression of our competitive instincts, instincts we project onto our God to justify such abominations as the war in Vietnam. If the second reading is true, Mailer is warning against *not* acting from such instincts, which represent the very core of reality, and it becomes then a real question as to why we should oppose the war. Surely it makes a critical difference which of these two views is correct, but how can we choose between them? The novel ends less than ten pages after D. J. experiences the presence of this God, and Mailer does nothing to clear up the scene's ambiguity. This may well be intended to illustrate Mailer's belief that we can never be absolutely certain whether it is God or the devil who "speaks" to us,[35] but what it tells us about the American character or the war in Vietnam is anybody's guess.

Similarly, the meaning of D. J.'s sexual repression is completely ambiguous. For Robert Langbaum, "The story suggests that the idyll ends in failure because the sexual experience to which it has been leading, an expression of bisexuality, is inhibited."[36] This would seem to agree with Mailer's exhortation to trust our instincts, formulated throughout his works in such pronouncements as the following: "Our emotions are a better guide to what goes on in these matters [sexual conception] than scientists" (*TPP*, 143); "if there is a strong ineradicable strain in human nature, one must not try to suppress it or anomaly, cancer, and plague will follow" (*TPP*, 22). Yet an equally imposing critic, Richard Poirier, remarks of D. J.'s relationship with Tex, "Their love for each other is a minority element already sickened by a homoerotic lust for masculine power. Such, in general, is Mailer's view of the possibilities of homosexual love, as in his writing about Genet in *The Prisoner of Sex* . . ."[37] As his last sentence makes clear, Poirier also takes his cue from Mailer's other works, in this case Mailer's many hostile statements concerning homosexuality. The novel's cryptic treatment of this episode has led its critics to seek external guidance as to Mailer's meaning, but even this has not prevented disagreements such as that between

Langbaum and Poirier; for the fact is that Mailer's discussions of homosexuality betray hopeless contradictions. Mailer opposes homosexuality because it is "unnatural," but praises the man who suppresses his homosexual instincts: "It was put best by Sartre who said that a homosexual is a man who practices homosexuality. A man who does not, is not homosexual—he is entitled to the dignity of his choice" (TPP, 243). This is to praise an act of will at the expense of instinct, precisely the opposite of what Mailer usually recommends.

The intellectual confusion at the end of Mailer's novel is of course devastating to its pretensions as an apologue. But then these pretensions have a similar effect on the entire novel as an action. I have no doubt that Mailer intended D. J.'s final efforts to achieve a redeeming authenticity as the climax to both his hero's personal plight and his own inquiry into America's role in Vietnam. In either case, however, we can only know that we are in the presence of failure, D. J.'s and/or America's. What kind of failure is altogether obscure. Insofar as D. J.'s fate fails to illumine the fate of America, the novel as apologue remains unresolved. Insofar as our attention is diverted to that larger, national issue, the novel as action loses much of its emotional power. Like An American Dream, Why Are We in Vietnam? teaches the hard lesson that it is easier to talk about combining different novelistic traditions than to achieve this end in a concrete fiction.

III Mailer's Marriage of Theory and Practice

I refer to talking about the fusion of novelistic traditions because Mailer has done just that in much of his recent literary criticism. Years ago Mailer could say that one of his early novels was about "a movie director and a girl with whom he had a bad affair" (Adv, 242), but this relatively humble fictional intention is alien to Mailer's literary discussions after 1959. The latter are invariably informed by the apocalyptic conception of the artist Mailer began to formulate in Advertisements for Myself. In that work Mailer tells us that the artist should be "as disturbing, as adventurous, as penetrating, as his energy and courage make possible" (Adv, 276); that "the final purpose of art is to intensify, even, if necessary, to exacerbate, the moral consciousness of people" (Adv, 384); that to turn "the consciousness of our time" is "an achievement which is the primary measure of a writer's size" (Adv, 465). No surprise, then, if Mailer used this work to publicize his new goal as a novelist: to create "a revolution in the consciousness of our time" (*Adv*, 17). This messianic conception of the writer's role is evident in almost everything Mailer has written since 1959. In 1966 he even went so far as to condemn Hemingway and Faulkner—"perhaps . . . the two greatest writers America ever had"—for refusing their chance to "save" America (*CC*, 99).

These quotations should suggest why Mailer has never again described his novels as "about" anything so trivial as their mere characters. Presumably one doesn't create a revolution in the consciousness of our time by telling stories which focus on a single unhappy love affair. Instead, one tells stories which reverberate with the largest implications for the nation's soul. In technical terms, one combines those American literary traditions we call *genteel* and *naturalistic*; one combines Edith Wharton's sense for detail with Dreiser's social/philosophical pretensions (see *CC*, 95-102). I have argued that in practice this leads to a hybrid which combines the forms of action and apologue. The point here is that this attempt grows directly out of Mailer's fictional theories, particularly his post-1959 belief that we should judge our novelists by their capacity to "clarify a nation's vision of itself" (*CC*, 98).

A writer so fiercely interested in ideas and their power to intensify our moral consciousness would be well advised, of course, to write the kind of fiction Robert Scholes has termed *fabulation*. As Scholes defines it, fabulation is a form essentially concerned with "ideas and ideals": "For the moment, suffice it to say that modern fabulation, like the ancient fabling of Aesop, tends away from the representation of reality but returns toward actual human life by way of ethically controlled fantasy. Many fabulators are allegorists. But the modern fabulators allegorize in peculiarly modern ways."[38] If I am right about Mailer's intentions and achievement, *An American Dream* and *Why Are We in Vietnam?* are the works of a late blooming fabulist whose allegorical methods are indeed peculiar because they presuppose that the representation of reality and ethically controlled fantasy are one and the same thing. This assumption is undercut by the works of Nabokov, Pynchon, and Barth, representative fabulists who seem intuitively to understand what Sacks has insisted upon in formal argument—that we can't have our cake and eat it too.

It will seem to many that in judging Mailer's recent novels I have exaggerated the importance of what Poirier calls "merely formal resolutions."[39] Poirier would protect the extraordinary passages in these novels against judgments based on mechanical concepts of form stressing neatness and symmetry. If we agree with Kenneth Burke, however, that "*Form* in literature is an arousing and fulfillment of desires. A work has form in so far as one part of it leads a reader to anticipate another part, to be gratified by the sequence,"[40] then we must reply that it isn't a lack of neatness we object to in Mailer's recent novels. Rather, it is the fact that expectations are constantly aroused only to be unfulfilled, as Mailer tries vainly to reconcile Dickens and Johnson. We don't protest formal irresolution per se, but the lack of significant form throughout. Mailer's early novels are superior to his later ones not only because they have satisfying resolutions, but because they achieve an emotional impact only possible if a work's parts so harmonize as to form a realized whole. It may be that Mailer himself is dimly aware of this, for he has not published a novel since 1967. This suggests that perhaps he has again felt the need to reconsider the assumptions underlying his fiction. At any rate, his major achievements for almost two decades now have been works of nonfiction, as we shall see in the chapters which follow.

CHAPTER 5

Mailer's Miscellanies: The Art of Self-Revelation

IT has become a commonplace—unavoidable at cocktail parties, student bars, even the dinner table—that Mailer's *real* achievement is to be found in his nonfiction. *There,* it is argued, we come upon Mailer "happily mired in reality, hobbled to the facts of time, place, self, as to an indispensable spouse of flesh and blood who continually saves him from his other self that yearns toward wasteful flirtations with *Spiritus Mundi.*"[1] If it seems a bit harsh to describe Mailer's novels as "wasteful flirtations with *Spiritus Mundi,*" many of us would still agree with Richard Foster's basic point: Mailer's nonfiction *is* a pleasant subject if one has any sympathy for his pretensions as a major writer. This is why it is curious that Mailer's much admired nonfiction should have generated so little critical commentary. From the attention it has received (or lack of it), one might think that Mailer's nonfiction was no more than artful journalism, as his enemies no doubt believe and his friends have failed to dispute.

Mailer has filled the breach himself, of course, arguing at every opportunity that his realistic nonfiction should not be confused with factual journalism. He has said recently that it is "the superb irony of his professional life" that he should receive the highest praise as a journalist, "for he knew he was not even a good journalist and possibly could not hold a top job if he had to turn in a story every day."[2] For Mailer, journalism is a matter of getting up factual reports intended for the mass media. It is an affair of *facts,* a ceaseless inquiry into who did what to whom, at what place and at what time. If he is not unreliable as a journalist, Mailer is hardly in competition with the daily reporter. In fact, the whole thrust of his nonfiction is away from "factual" history. "For once let us try to think about a political convention without losing ourselves in housing projects of fact and issue." So Mailer begins his first important essay of the 1960s, "Superman Comes to the Supermarket" (*TPP*, 27). Mailer would replace housing projects of fact and issue with a sense for the mysteries of personality and the relations among such mysteries (interests obviously taken over from the house of fiction). He has written that "there is no history without nuance,"[3] and finally this defines his goal as a "journalist": to capture the nuances of recent American experience and so define its true, as opposed to its *statistical*, meaning.[4]

The concern for nuance and the rejection of "fact" have led of course to Mailer's "engaged" reportage—have led to a literary form closer to the novel than to traditional reporting. This form is best embodied in *The Armies of the Night* (1968), Mailer's first extended foray into the political history of our time. It is also to be seen in his more recent works: *Miami and the Siege of Chicago* (1968), *Of a Fire on the Moon* (1970), *The Prisoner of Sex* (1971), *St. George and the Godfather* (1972), *Marilyn* (1973), and *The Fight* (1975). Contrary to a widely held opinion, however, these books did not come to us as unanticipated and unique achievements. As early as 1959 Mailer began to make the nonfictional innovations which made his recent works possible. I want to consider this early work here, both as the preparation for Mailer's writings after 1967 and as an independent achievement which deserves more attention than it has yet received. By tracing the gradual emergence of Mailer's "subjective" approach to nonfiction, we should come to see what A. Alvarez meant when he said that Mailer's early essays now seemed "like so many training flights" for *The Armies of the Night*.[5] But we should also come to see that as Mailer turned more and more to using the techniques of fiction in the essay form he was able to succeed in that form as never before. This is no mean achievement—among his contemporaries only James Baldwin has surpassed Mailer as an essayist.

It is usually assumed that Mailer's nonfiction has been received more generously than his fiction; but this isn't obvious to anyone who reads through the reviews of Mailer's early collections. Presumably the people who now speak of Mailer's "brilliant" journalism weren't available to review *Advertisements for Myself, The Presidential Papers*, and *Cannibals and Christians*.[6] What the reviewers failed to do, Mailer's admirers continue to neglect: discuss the collections as something more than compilations. While the best case for Mailer's nonfiction is not to be made in arguing that the collections are unified wholes, Mailer's efforts to give them unity should be acknowledged.

They reveal Mailer's fascinating attempt to make art by juxtaposing his most brilliant and ephemeral pieces. They bespeak his literary courage if not his common sense.

I *The First Three Collections*

Mailer once referred to his "optimistic love affair with the secret potentialities of this nation" (*CC*, 71), as if to acknowledge that his argument with America has been a lover's quarrel. This quarrel is at the heart of Mailer's first collection, *Advertisements for Myself* (1959), a sermon delivered to America by a troubled American, as Mailer's rhetoric constantly reminds us: "So, yes, it may be time to say that the Republic is in real peril, and we are the cowards who must defend courage, sex, consciousness, the beauty of the body, the search for love, and the capture of what may be, after all, an heroic destiny" (*Adv*, 23-24). A few pages earlier Mailer has remarked that "the shits are killing us" (*Adv*, 19). Thus the sense of urgency in the lines quoted above. Thus *Advertisements for Myself,* a book which explores the many ways in which the "shits" are killing us (or, at the very least, how they are killing one of us). As such it is a work of social criticism in which Mailer is his own first (and last) example. But of course *Advertisements* is many other things as well: an exercise in personal therapy, an act of propaganda, a "muted autobiography" (*Adv*, 335), and what I will later define as a literary autobiography. *Advertisements* is any and all of these things because its materials are so diverse. Mailer reprints whole or in selection *everything* that he wrote prior to 1959: fiction, essays and articles, journalism, interviews, poetry, plays (fragments thereof), and autobiography (some would say confession). Whatever the principle of selection at work in the making of *Advertisements*, it was not quality alone. The first question about this book must be whether it has any artistic unity whatsoever.

Mailer's better critics have "explained" *Advertisements* on the theory that Mailer used the book as literary or personal therapy. According to Barry Leeds, "The process of establishing an ordered form within which to present the various pieces which make up *Advertisements* was a project intended to provide Mailer with a clearer view of what he had done and what he wished yet to do in his writing."[7] Thus we are told by Donald Kaufmann, "Mailer is writing as much for himself as for his readers. Mailer in effect is serving as his own therapist . . ."[8] Now, Mailer is not above using his writing for therapeutic ends, as he reveals in his discussion of the weekly column he once wrote for *The Village Voice*: "So my readers suffered through more than one week, while the column served as therapy for me: I was eliminating some of the sludge of the past. My style then came into being out of no necessity finer than a purgative to bad habit" (*Adv*, 283). But even if we assume that *Advertisements* was such a purgative, how does this advance our investigation into the artistic principles which unify the work? This approach simply skirts the issue entirely and assumes that *Advertisements* can only be explained as a "solution" to its author's personal problems. If we look to the work and not the author, we should do rather better than this.

Advertisements may not be an unappreciated masterpiece, but its pieces and parts do fit into several complementary patterns. The first of these is frankly propagandistic. At one point Mailer explains that *Advertisements* is an attempt to keep his name before the public and set the stage for a major novel to which he will devote the next ten years of his life: "If it is to have any effect, and I can hardly look forward to exhausting the next ten years without hope of a deep explosion of effect, the book will be fired to its fuse by the rumor that once I pointed to the farthest fence and said that within ten years I would try to hit the longest ball ever to go up into the accelerated hurricane air of our American letters" (*Adv*, 477). In one sense, then, *Advertisements* is literally an advertisement. The reader is invited to sample Mailer's previous work and several selections from his next novel (its prologue, a poem by one of its characters, and "The Time of Her Time"). On this basis, he is to await The Great American Novel which Mailer will soon be offering to an alerted public. Understood in this light, *Advertisements* has no great claim on literary immortality. Mailer hasn't even published his advertised masterpiece; like many advertisers, he has promised rather more than he has delivered.

Apart from its role in Mailer's public relations, however, *Advertisements* is obviously a kind of autobiography. Mailer introduces each of his pieces with commentary he calls "advertisements," and these sections form, in Mailer's words, the "muted autobiography of the near-beat adventurer who was myself" (*Adv*, 335). Mailer's commentary is what his critics reviewed when *Advertisements* was first published. According to his reviewers, Mailer stood revealed as "a literary terrorist" and "a dotty messiah," and his book as a whole confirmed nothing less than his "artistic crack-up."[9] The reviewers give the impression that Mailer's commentary is the least attractive part of *Advertisements*. However, I would agree with Mailer who says in a prefatory note that "he tried to make the advertisements more readable than the rest of his pages" (*Adv*, 7). It seems to me that he has succeeded. What he hasn't done is write a true autobiography. While all the advertisements reveal something about their author, only a few sections of the book tell us much about Mailer's personal life. Like Fitzgerald's *The Crack-Up*, *Advertisements* includes autobiographical materials without becoming a traditional autobiography. As Mailer says early in the book, "It is most certainly not my aim to make this a thoroughgoing autobiography" (*Adv*, 107).

Advertisements is more aptly described as a *literary* autobiography.[10] Mailer makes this clear about two-thirds of the way into his book: "In 'The White Negro,' in 'The Time of Her Time,' and in 'Advertisements for Myself on the Way Out' can be found the real end of this muted autobiography . . . With these three seeds, let us say the book has its end" (*Adv*, 335). *Advertisements* is a biography of the *writer* Norman Mailer. It is an illustrated chronicle of this writer's search for his true role as an artist. Its final sections reveal the climax to this search as Mailer comes upon the subject of Hip. Because Hip is to furnish the material for his projected masterpiece, Mailer can also use these sections to cap his self-advertisement. But insofar as all the materials in the book are related, these final "seeds" are evidence that the writer's artistic voyage has been successful.

This structure gives Mailer's book unity but it is ultimately self-defeating. It allows Mailer to include anything he wants to include: stories written in college, stories he couldn't previously publish, political essays he admits are "on the tiresome side" (*Adv*, 186), essays he describes as "no more than expanded notes" (*Adv*, 390). These pieces do illustrate Mailer's several literary directions prior to his present course, but they are also unmistakably dull and inherently valueless. Mailer was not unaware of the problem. In the "Advertisement for Part Three" he writes, "This next part of the collection is put together almost entirely of writings on the fly. They are superficial, off-balance, too personal at times, not very agreeable. There would be little excuse for including such bits if I had not decided to use my personality as the armature of this book" (*Adv*, 219). Alas, there are too many such "bits" in *Advertisements*, too many articles, poems, fragments, and fragments of fragments which can only interest those of us fascinated by Norman Mailer. The form Mailer gave to *Advertisements* is too much a rationalization for reprinting juvenilia, false starts, and since abandoned projects. These pieces do set off the later, more mature essays and stories—if the reader gets to these later selections. Though it includes such fine things as "The White Negro," "The Man Who Studied Yoga," and "The Time of Her Time," *Advertisements* is finally a book for Mailer's fans.

The Presidential Papers (1963) suffers from much the same defect. In this second of his miscellanies, Mailer again resorts to a "defense for the superficial" (*TPP*, 99) in order to justify some of the material he has chosen to reprint. This time around, however, there is less need for such a defense. Except for the so-called poems and the concluding philosophical dialogue, "The Metaphysics of the Belly," the individual pieces in this collection are excellent. Even the brief columns from *Esquire* and *Commentary* are of greater intrinsic interest than columns from *The Village Voice* reprinted in *Advertisements;* even the open letters to Kennedy and Castro are readable.

At the beginning of *The Presidential Papers,* Mailer again tries to persuade us that his various materials are intimately related. In this case Mailer's personality is not the "armature" of his book; instead its focal point is John F. Kennedy, archetype of the modern hero (or potential hero). Mailer tells us that *The Presidential Papers* was written for Kennedy's benefit. The various selections are included "because their subject matter is fit concern for a President." Mailer adopts the pose of "a court wit, an amateur advisor" (*TPP*, 1), who brings together in his collection writings about and for President Kennedy, a man who has every virtue but one—imagination (*TPP*, 3). Mailer offers himself as Kennedy's imagination. He would introduce the President to the principle of existential politics, an imaginative principle for which Kennedy has great need.

The skeptical will reply that *The Presidential Papers* includes very little that is "fit concern for a President." While he takes up such issues as juvenile delinquency, the Negro emergence, the CIA, and totalitarianism, Mailer also deals with the nature of dread, the dialectic of God and the devil, sex of upper classes and lower classes, cannibalism, and digestion and the unconscious. (These are among the "topics" Mailer lists at the beginning of his book—*TPP*, 7.) Moreover, he deals with all of these subjects in much the same way. His method is notoriously impressionistic—a most unpolitical method. But for Mailer this is precisely what recommends his book to a man like Kennedy. He argues that the President has for too long dealt with the same old issues in the most "objective" manner possible. Kennedy suffers from "intellectual malnutrition" because he has been given "predigested" information (*TPP*, 1, 2); he needs a different kind of advisor, for he is now offered "not nuances but facts" (*TPP*, 2). Again, Mailer's aim is to offer nuance wherever he finds it—in the processes of digestion as well as the architectural style of urban renewal. For nuance *is* reality, and politics ought to deal with reality. The President—by extension, all of us—should begin to concern himself with the realities of our situation, even if these realities are not traditionally political. He should come to appreciate the fine lesson of existential politics: "Existential politics is simple. It has a basic argument: if there is a strong ineradicable strain in human nature, one must not try to suppress it or anomaly, cancer, and plague will follow. Instead one must find an art into which it can grow" (*TPP*, 22).

The Presidential Papers charts the anomaly, cancer, and plague which have come to America and proposes a number of solutions, all based on the principle that we must not suppress our desires but rather channel them into artful activities. There is a real thematic consistency running through the book's separate pieces, as Mailer takes up different features of his old enemy, "technology land" ("A tasteless, sexless, odorless sanctity in architecture, manners, modes, styles"—*TPP*, 43). Those pieces not concerned with describing our descent into plague offer a solution to this drift. (This is most obviously the case in Mailer's long essay on Kennedy, "Superman Comes to the Supermarket.") When Mailer writes that "totalitarianism has been the continuing preoccupation of this book" (*TPP*, 175), we must grant the implicit claim that this book is sufficiently of a piece to have a continuing preoccupation. Using the figure of Kennedy to represent America—much potential marred by too little imagination, too little insight—Mailer has produced a volume almost worthy of the promotion on its paperback cover: "a brilliant, slashing portrait of the Kennedy years by the most controversial writer of our time."

Not everyone would agree, of course. Many of his reviewers seemed to think that Mailer had betrayed the muse by turning from the novel to publish what one reviewer termed "a collection of magazine pieces . . . essentially the oddments turned out by a novelist who is not writing a novel."[11] Richard Gilman stated outright what many other reviewers hinted in so many ways—that Mailer had abandoned art in pursuit of his "naive and addled philosophical bases."[12] There was no one to reply that in such essays as "Superman

Comes to the Supermarket" and "Ten Thousand Words a Minute"
Mailer had in many ways *advanced* his art. There was no one to
suggest that perhaps Mailer was onto something with his "unprofes-
sional" approach to our social and political life. In fact, as we will see
in reviewing the growth of Mailer's nonfictional techniques, *The
Presidential Papers* includes more of Mailer's successful essays than
any other of his collections.

It is more than a little ironic, then, that *Cannibals and Christians*
(1966), Mailer's next collection, received a much better press; for
Cannibals is almost certainly the least successful of Mailer's first
three miscellanies. The book consists in part of articles written in the
early 1960s but not collected in *The Presidential Papers*. It includes
one selection, "The Metaphysics of the Belly," which is reprinted
from *The Presidential Papers* as an introduction to its sequel, "The
Political Economy of Time." *Cannibals* is therefore burdened with
not one but *two* of Mailer's "philosophical" dialogues. (Indeed, if we
count the brief "The First Day's Interview," there are *three* such
dialogues.) Mailer has also seen fit to publish more of his poems.[13] He
refers to them here as "short hairs," and explains that they are
interspersed throughout *Cannibals* as "seasoning" (*CC*, xii). These
"short hairs" take up no less than sixty-seven pages altogether, and
Cannibals would have to be a very great book indeed to overcome
such uninspired "seasoning." Moreover, *Cannibals* suffers when
compared with the earlier collections because it simply includes
fewer interesting selections. The political writings of part one are
especially unexciting if set beside comparable essays in *The Presidential Papers*; and Mailer's "philosophical dialogues" must have been
read from beginning to end by myself and a dozen other academics at
work on Mailer. *Cannibals* sometimes reminds one of a graveyard for
Mailer memorabilia.

Yet Mailer argues that the separate pieces in *Cannibals* "have
relations with one another . . . the writings are parts of a continuing
and more or less comprehensive vision of existence into which
everything must fit" (*CC*, xi). These "relations" are sometimes
obscure (e.g., the thematic connection between Goldwater's nomination and the emergence of Camp). Occasionally they are simply
spurious. For example, Mailer begins an essay on the history of
American literature by remarking, "There has been a war at the
center of American letters for a long time" (*CC*, 95). Presumably this
"war" is related to the struggle between Cannibal and Christian

which Mailer sees as the latest stage in our dialectical evolution. But he is in fact referring to the "war" between naturalism and the genteel tradition. Only a relations hunter *extraordinaire* could see this war as one version of the Cannibal/Christian dialectic. Like most of the literary criticism in *Cannibals*, this essay has only a nodding acquaintance with the book's announced theme.

This theme—the war between Cannibal and Christian in contemporary America—does inform much of the book, however. Mailer's penchant for the dialectical has been obvious since *Advertisements*, where he develops the contrast between the hipster and the White Protestant whose "ultimate sympathy must be with science, factology, and committee rather than sex, birth, heat, flesh, creation, the sweet and the funky," the provinces of Hip (*Adv*, 388). In *The Presidential Papers*, Mailer came to see this conflict as rather more universal, as we see in the passage already quoted in chapter four which describes America's "double life," of politics as well as "untapped, ferocious, lonely and romantic desires, that concentration of ecstasy and violence which is the dream life of the nation" (*TPP*, 38). In *Cannibals and Christians*, as the title implies, Mailer returns to this notion of America's dialectical development as embodied by his "Cannibals" and "Christians." The "Cannibals" are the rightwing of our political life, obsessed with the "second-rate" in America and confident that "one can save the world by killing off what is second-rate." The "Christians" are not to be found in Christian churches. They cut across the political spectrum from moderate Republicans to Communists, united by their belief that "science is the salvation of ill" and "death is the end of discussion." Humanitarian and pacifistic, these Christians have nonetheless succeeded in "starting all the wars of our own time, since every war since the Second World War has been initiated by liberals or Communists." The Cannibals are no less paradoxical, for if they "think of Jesus as Love," they also "get an erection from the thought of whippings, blood, burning crosses, burning bodies, and screams in mass graves"—the Cannibals are not irrelevant to Vietnam (*CC*, 4). Mailer finds both groups unappealing: "Sellah, sellah—is it better to be a foul old Cannibal or a Christian dying of nausea?" (*CC*, 91).

Mailer's Cannibal/Christian dichotomy is only the most recent attempt in his miscellanies to explain the social illness of America. In *Advertisements* he rails against "national conformity" (*Adv*, 283). In *The Presidential Papers* he protests the many forms of totalitarianism which have come to America. *Cannibals* is the logical result of Mailer's growing pessimism, evident in the shifting terms of his protest. What he first attacked as conformity and then as totalitarianism, he now refers to as a plague: ". . . it has been the continuing obsession of this writer that the world is entering a time of plague" (*CC*, 2). Once again Mailer's subject is America-in-plague. Only now there is no antidote. No case is made in *Cannibals* for "the creative nihilism of the Hip" (*Adv*, 325); there is no brief for "existential politics" (*TPP*, 22, 43). Now there is only a lament for the devastation we have brought upon ourselves.

The lament in *Cannibals* is profoundly conservative, and thus marks a real transition to Mailer's more recent writings. In 1968 Mailer would refer to himself as a left conservative,[14] but already in *Cannibals* the exrevolutionary socialist has replaced Marx with Edmund Burke; already he is writing that "1964 was also a year in which a real conservative still had a great deal to say to the nation" (*CC*, 47). This real conservative is Mailer himself, and what he says to the nation is worthy of Burke: "There seems at loose an impulse to uproot every vestige of the past, an urge so powerful one wonders if it is not with purpose, if it is not in the nature of twentieth-century man to uproot himself not only from his past, but from his planet" (*CC*, 235). It is the tragedy of this collection that only in the essay on Goldwater does Mailer lift his lament to the level of art. There is art to the several literary articles; but these selections are not connected to the volume's fundamental theme. Much of what remains is fragmentary or even trivial.

Mailer's miscellanies are simply too heterogeneous to reward his efforts to make of them unified wholes (*The Presidential Papers* is perhaps an exception). The fiction in the collections is not up to the standard of Mailer's novels; much of the nonfiction is occasional in the extreme. Hostile critics might say that *most* of the selections, not just a few political essays, read as if they were "no more than expanded notes." But this is only to say that Mailer's worst work does not measure up to his best. Lodged in his first three miscellanies are some of Mailer's most accomplished performances. Collectively these essays form a rather slim volume—slimmer than any of the published collections. But the volume I envisage is one of the more significant works in contemporary American literature. It includes the best of Mailer's early nonfiction—again, except for James Baldwin's essays, the best nonfiction we have had in the postwar period. Among Mailer's collections, it is this hypothetical gathering of his better pieces which should be considered in detail.

II   *The Early Essays*

This hypothetical volume would include a moderate variety of materials, but not the great variety of Mailer's published miscellanies. Missing would be the interviews and self-interviews, open letters to Castro and correspondence with the editor of the *New York Review of Books*, refutation of a gossip columnist, therapeutic columns for *The Village Voice*, remarks on the sexual implications of the T-formation, among others. If variety is the spice of life, mediocrity is the death of attention. Our ideal volume would be limited to the introductory materials written especially for the first three collections, much of the literary criticism, and those essays published after *Advertisements* which focus on specific American events (e.g., political conventions, championship fights, televised tours of the White House).[15] I agree with the critical consensus that Mailer's reputation as a "journalist" rests largely on the last mentioned items. His essays on the political conventions of 1960 and 1964, his essay on Jackie Kennedy, and his coverage of the first Patterson-Liston fight seem to me by far the most impressive items in his early nonfiction. To this list we must add only one earlier piece, "The White Negro," to have fully fleshed out our hypothetical volume of Mailer's better essays. Because these essays range from 1957 to the early 1960s, they should allow us to trace the growth of Mailer's unique approach to nonfiction.

Like their author, Mailer's political and social essays have changed remarkably over the years. The pieces which go back to the 1950s hardly anticipate the essayist who will brood over psychic forces at work in a championship prize fight; whether their subject is David Riesman, homosexuality, Marx, or Sputnik, they all betray the true identity of the radical intellectual who once dissected western defense for readers of *Dissent*. Significantly, Mailer has all but repudiated his earliest essays: ". . . whenever I sat down to do an article, I seemed to thicken in the throat as I worded my sentences and my rhetoric felt shaped by the bad political prose of our years" (*Adv*, 186). Indeed, such essays as "The Meaning of Western Defense," "David Riesman Reconsidered," and "The Homosexual Villain" are unpleasant reading for anyone who admires Mailer's prose style. Since collected in *Advertisements*, these articles suggest that Mailer has no real gift for the closely reasoned and "objective" analytical essay. Mailer seems to have recognized this himself, for his nonfiction has become increasingly less analytical with each year.

"The White Negro" (1957) is Mailer's one significant essay of this early period. In one sense an almost scholarly discussion of the hipster, this piece succeeds where Mailer's other early essays do not because it goes beyond the analysis of a cultural or political situation to create what Mailer has called a sociological "fiction" (*Adv*, 196). Mailer's "fiction"—of the hipster as revolutionary elitist—is not, of course, a wholly imaginative creation. Mailer tries to describe a real phenomenon with real historical roots. He traces the birth of the hipster to the catastrophes of the twentieth century and views this figure as a rebel against society—that "collective creation" revealed by World War II to be "murderous" and by the postwar era to be suffering from "a collective failure of nerve" (*Adv*, 338). He is also careful to identify the source of the hipster's life style—that Negro culture based on jazz, marijuana, and sexuality (hence Mailer's title; see *Adv*, 340-41, 348). But starting with these observations on the hipster's genesis, Mailer is quick to take up a partisan defense of the hipster's intuitions. The real thrust of his "analysis" is not descriptive but prophetic. The hipster is seen as the "dangerous front-runner of a new kind of personality which could become the central expression of human nature before the twentieth century is over" (*Adv*, 345). The more inspired passages in "The White Negro" always reject the generally analytical tone of the essay for a more lyrical evocation of the new hero who has come among us. The following passage is representative:

> It is this knowledge which provides the curious community of feeling in the world of the hipster, a muted cool religious revival to be sure, but the element which is exciting, disturbing, nightmarish perhaps, is that incompatibles have come to bed, the inner life and the violent life, the orgy and the dream of love, the desire to murder and the desire to create, a dialectical conception of existence with a lust for power, a dark, romantic, and yet undeniably dynamic view of existence for it sees every man and woman as moving individually through each moment of life forward into growth or backward into death. (*Adv*, 342-43)

The "knowledge" Mailer refers to is the hipster's supposed awareness of what is good or bad for his own psyche. Mailer begins by remarking on this "knowledge" and ends with nothing less than a claim for the hipster's "dialectical conception of existence." Jean Malaquais has called this claim "a gorgeous flower of Mailer's romantic idealism" (*Adv*, 362), and I doubt that many of us would disagree. Insofar as "The White Negro" is sociology as we tend to think of it, Mailer's achievement is limited by such excessive claims for his subject. But "The White Negro" is really a lyrical defense of Mailer's conversion to Hip, an American existentialism which differs from the French variety because it is based on "a mysticism of the flesh" rather than "the rationality of French existentialism" (*Adv*, 314). Mailer succeeds in "The White Negro" to the degree he persuades us that Hip has "a dark, romantic, and yet undeniably dynamic view of existence," rather than that it is literally derived from Black culture or is a major social force. Despite its sometimes ponderous tone, "The White Negro" should therefore be viewed as not so altogether different from Mailer's more recent essays. Like these essays, it is distinguished by the quality of Mailer's brooding and most partisan reflections on what he has observed.

If "The White Negro" was an advance, the real turning point for Mailer's nonfiction was *Advertisements for Myself*. After 1959 Mailer's essays are marked by the strong personal voice he developed in writing the "advertisements" for his first collection. At first the difference is only stylistic, as Mailer cultivates this personal voice and so avoids the "thickening" in the throat which came to him while writing those political essays influenced by "early, passionate, and injudicious reading of the worst sort of Max Lernerish liberal junk" (*Adv*, 186). But gradually Mailer did much more than this; he came to introduce into his "journalism" not only a personal voice but his personality as well. His writings from 1960 to 1968 represent a continuing effort to focus his explorations into recent American history by transforming this personal element into a functional persona.

Before he could do this, however, Mailer had to discover the value of fictional techniques for a work of nonfiction. He seems to have made this discovery in "Superman Comes to the Supermarket" (1960). Ostensibly a report on the 1960 Democratic convention, this essay is really a glorification of John Fitzgerald Kennedy, the convention's nominee. Mailer has acknowledged the highly partisan, even prop-agandistic character of the piece: "I was forcing a reality, I was bending reality like a field of space to curve the time I wished to create. I was not writing with the hope that perchance I could find reality by being sufficiently honest to perceive it, but on the contrary was distorting reality in the hope that thereby I could affect it. I was engaging in an act of propaganda" (*TPP*, 60). In other words, Mailer was trying to get Jack Kennedy elected. "Superman Comes to the Supermarket" first appeared several weeks before the 1960 election (*Esquire*, November 1960), and Mailer's hidden purpose was to encourage unenthusiastic Democrats to vote for Kennedy. Mailer believes that he was successful; he thinks that, as much as anyone, he deserves the credit for Kennedy's narrow victory (*TPP*, 60-61, 88-89). Disregarding this claim—the merciful thing to do—we can say that Mailer's covert intentions do not discredit his essay as literature. Mailer's partisanship here is similar to his position vis-a-vis the hipster in "The White Negro" where his enthusiasm for his subject also generated some of his finest prose.

Impressed by Kennedy's charisma rather than his politics (which were traditionally liberal, if not a bit conservative), Mailer set out to dramatize the mysterious allure of Kennedy's personality. Toward this end he employed numerous literary devices, most of them novelistic: character analysis, character sketches, shifts in chronology, the juxtaposition of contrasting characters and events, etc. But his first tool was sheer rhetoric. He remarks at the beginning of his essay that he will "dress" his argument in "a ribbon or two of metaphor" (*TPP*, 28), and the "argument" is indeed metaphorical. Kennedy is variously described as "a great box-office actor," "a hero central to his time," and "a prince in the unstated aristocracy of the American dream" (*TPP*, 38, 41, 59); he is said to have "a patina of that other life, the second American life, the long electric night with the fires of neon leading down the highway to the murmur of jazz" (*TPP*, 31). Kennedy is contrasted throughout with the sort of candidate desired by the bosses of the convention—the totally political, totally predictable candidate such as Richard Nixon or Richard Daley. Mailer laments that we have embraced the security of Eisenhower and become technology land itself. We are a country of mythical heroes, but our faith in such heroes has burned out. We are therefore in need of a Kennedy, an American prince who will rekindle our faith in the American dream. The nation will reveal itself by its selection of Kennedy or Nixon: "One would have an inkling at last if the desire of America was for drama or stability, for adventure or monotony" (*TPP*, 58). Will the American people be so courageous as to embrace their own lonely and romantic desires?

Needless to say, the "argument" here is some distance removed from "fact and issue." It is a novelist's argument, and throughout

"Superman Comes to the Supermarket" Mailer performs the good novelist's task of heightening his protagonist by treating everything else in a manner which can only set off Kennedy's contrasting excellence. The scene at the convention is described so as to make Kennedy appear not only by contrast a matinee idol, but a saviour come unto heathens as well. Los Angeles is "a kingdom of stucco, the playground for mass men"; the Biltmore Hotel, convention headquarters, is "one of the ugliest hotels in the world" (*TPP*, 33). The people at the convention are either political hacks or such party professionals as Lyndon Baines Johnson ("when he smiled the corners of his mouth squeezed gloom; when he was pious, his eyes twinkled irony; when he spoke in a righteous tone, he looked corrupt"—*TPP*, 35). It is to *this* city, *this* hotel, and *these* people that Kennedy comes, the movie star come to the palace to claim the princess (*TPP*, 38). Mailer also places in evidence Nixon's incredibly mawkish remarks upon receiving the Republican nomination: " 'Yes, I want to say,' said Nixon, 'that whatever abilities I have, I got from my mother . . . and my father . . . and my school and my church' " (*TPP*, 45). He dismisses with contempt the Republican convention which followed and offers yet another judgment on that convention's nominee: "The apocalyptic hour of Uriah Heep" (*TPP*, 58). He describes in detail Adlai Stevenson's presence at the Democratic convention, for Stevenson plays the passive antihero to Kennedy's hero (*TPP*, 50-51). The "events" Mailer chose to describe in this essay were selected by a professional novelist, not a political journalist. The very texture of his essay validates Mailer's attractive "creation" of John Kennedy—a creation soon adopted by the country at large.

"Superman Comes to the Supermarket" reveals the novelist's hand, then, but it does not include the device most characteristic of Mailer's recent nonfiction—the use of himself as participant as well as spectator. For this we must look to the later essays, beginning with Mailer's second convention piece, "In The Red Light: A History of the Republican Convention in 1964." As its subtitle suggests, "In The Red Light" is about the Republican convention rather than its leading man. (Goldwater, its most important figure, is hardly the hero of the piece.) The essay is formally divided into three parts: a history of events prior to the convention, including Goldwater's rise to power in the Republican party; a description of the convention up to Goldwater's nomination; and a spectator's views on Goldwater's acceptance speech. Only at the end does Mailer abandon the pose of reporter to reflect on Goldwater's ascendancy and the state of the union in this year of Johnson versus Goldwater. Yet Mailer's interpretive presence is felt throughout. It is this "presence" which distinguishes "In The Red Light" from journalistic accounts of the convention.

Mailer's role in the essay begins to emerge in the political portraits of part two. Here Everett Dirksen is seen as "an old organist who could play all the squeaks in all the stops, rustle over all the dead bones of all the dead mice in all the pipes," and we can *hear* Dirksen as Mailer describes him, "making a sound like the whir of the air conditioning in a two-mile tunnel" (*CC*, 34). And once we have read Mailer's description of George Romney as "a handsome version of Boris Karloff, all honesty, big-jawed, soft-eyed, eighty days at sea on a cockeyed passion" (*CC*, 31), we can never see Romney again without visions of Frankenstein. These examples suggest that Mailer is not exactly a disinterested historian, as is most obvious from his "analysis" of the Goldwater crusade. Goldwater delegates are presented as "a Wasp Mafia where the grapes of wrath were stored" (*CC*, 16); they are seen as "a frustrated posse, a convention of hangmen who subscribe to the principle that the executioner has his rights as well" (*CC*, 27); their representatives in the California delegation are said to resemble Robert Mitchum playing the mad reverend in *Night of the Hunter* (*CC*, 36). Mailer even senses this fanaticism in the bagpipers who play throughout the convention, for theirs is "the true music of the Wasps" in which we detect "the Faustian rage of a white civilization . . . the cry of a race which was born to dominate and might never learn to share" (*CC*, 25). Mailer's metaphorical rendering of the convention might be charged with bias, but many of us will sympathize with the underlying assumption: that what really happened at the convention can be best captured only by a voice concerned with human acts and belonging to a human speaker. Even where Mailer is on shakiest ground as a reporter—his characterizations—most of us will probably admit that *his* Scranton, Goldwater, or Eisenhower at least suggests the man we all observe rather than the faceless political "figure" we encounter in the newspapers. But the point is perhaps obvious. Dealing with the convention as he would in a novel, Mailer achieves the same imaginative authority in what is formally an essay.

Mailer's impressionism is justified because "In The Red Light" is about his response to the ascending right wing rather than the phenomenon itself. Mailer attaches such weight to his impressions because he assumes they are representative. They are also terribly ambivalent, which accounts for the dramatic tension so characteristic of "In The Red Light." The Goldwaterites may impress Mailer as a Wasp Mafia, but their demonstration for Goldwater suggests something about their "inner condition" which is both more ominous and more appealing:

There was an unmistakable air of beauty, as if a rainbow had come to a field of war, or Goths around a fire saw visions in a cave. The heart of the beast had loosed a primitive call. Civilization was worn thin in the center and to the Left the black man raised his primitive cry; now to the Right were the maniacal blue eyes of the other primitive. The jungles and the forests were readying for war. For a moment, beauty was there—it is always there as tribes and clans gather for war (*CC*, 34).

The appeal in this is suggested earlier when Mailer remarks, "I had been leading a life which was a trifle too pointless and a trifle too full of guilt and my gullet was close to nausea with the endless compromises of an empty liberal center. So I followed the four days of the convention with something more than simple apprehension" (*CC*, 26). This passage goes far to explain Mailer's fascination with Goldwater, for Goldwater is an answer to the empty liberal center. Finally, of course, he is an unacceptable answer ("He was humbug . . . Goldwater was a demagogue"—*CC*, 40), but he does provide Mailer with a rather ominous clue to our condition as a people. For if men like Mailer feel the attraction of a Goldwater, then Mailer's conclusion is probably true: "America has come to a point from which she will never return. The wars are coming and the deep revolutions of the soul" (*CC*, 45). Mailer has rendered the convention so persuasively, such prophecies almost seem inevitable.

We can be grateful for Mailer's fascination with Goldwater—his account of the Republican convention is much richer than it might otherwise have been. Elsewhere, however, Mailer has used his own personality not only to focus coverage of an event or movement but also as his basic subject. He has treated himself as a character in one of his novels might be treated, and so brought the essay form to the borders of fiction. Consider "An Evening with Jackie Kennedy, or, The Wild West of the East" (1962). The final section of this essay reads much like "In The Red Light," for Mailer first describes Jackie Kennedy's televised tour of the White House, then uses the occasion to speculate on the depressing condition of America and what Mrs. Kennedy might be able to do about it if she were somewhat less "phony" (*TPP*, 97). But the final section is no more than one-third of the essay. By first reporting his personal encounters with Mrs.

Kennedy, Mailer places in evidence his initial impressions of the First Lady; but he also provides a portrait of Norman Mailer, necessary, he implies, if his criticisms of Jackie Kennedy are to be fairly assessed by his readers (*TPP*, 88). It is this self-portrait which is original in "An Evening with Jackie Kennedy." Mailer dramatizes not only his initial conversation with Mrs. Kennedy but also the domestic details surrounding it, from an argument with his wife the day he is to interview the Kennedys to his wife's conversation with Jackie Kennedy the next day (*TPP*, 84, 87). Here Mailer writes about himself with real comic detachment, observing that he was in a "Napoleonic mood" at the time he received a letter from Jackie Kennedy, noting that he replied "in the cadence of a Goethe" (*TPP*, 87).

Not that self-deprecation is the essence of Mailer's self-portrait. Mailer is typically earnest when it comes to representing his own ideas; he has even admitted that the middle section of this essay is "needlessly long and close to comic in its intensity, for it sails under a full head of sermon."[16] Moreover, much of the personal material is used to introduce his meetings and correspondence with Jackie Kennedy, still the essay's subject. Nonetheless, we have here the beginnings of Mailer's more recent, more objective self-portraiture—Mailer with irony, so to speak. The emphasis on Mailer's interaction with his subject anticipates the strategy of his more recent nonfiction.

This strategy is most successfully employed in "Ten Thousand Words a Minute" (1962), Mailer's account of the first Patterson-Liston fight. Here Mailer emphasizes his own role in a public event almost to the exclusion of the event itself. He may have hit upon this strategy through necessity rather than choice, for the fight itself was a one round "fiasco" (*TPP*, 307). In any case, Mailer's title is a sly hint that he is concerned here with something more than the coverage of a championship fight. Mailer has indeed written nearly twenty-thousand words about a two-minute fight—*and* what he takes to be its symbolic meaning, his relation to it that week in Chicago, and his reactions to its outcome. These latter concerns are what justify the length of "Ten Thousand Words a Minute," the longest and the best of Mailer's essays.

I don't mean to suggest that Mailer has neglected his duties as a reporter. In part one he gives a fascinating account of the men surrounding the two fighters; in part two he offers a very professional report on the Patterson and Liston training camps; in part three he presents what must be the most vivid published account of the fight itself; and in part four he manages to cover all the post-fight activities, including Liston's press conference the next day. Impressive as Mailer's reportage can be, however, "Ten Thousand Words a Minute" is still about Norman Mailer's coverage of a prize fight rather than the fight itself. We sense this as early as part two, where Mailer dramatizes not only his observations of Patterson and Liston but also his conversations with such men as Cus D'Amato, Patterson's manager, and Jim Jacobs, Patterson's public relations assistant. The humor here is at Mailer's expense; like the self-deprecating passages in "An Evening with Jackie Kennedy," it expresses some of the same ironic self-characterization so crucial to the success of *The Armies of the Night*. For that matter, the humor is important here. "Ten Thousand Words a Minute" offers Mailer's symbolic reading of the Patterson-Liston fight, with Liston as Faust and Patterson as the archetypal underdog; with Liston as Sex and Patterson as Love; with Liston as the hustler and Patterson, the artist; with Liston as the devil and Patterson as God (*TPP*, 255). Such weighty identifications are presented in all metaphoric seriousness. Like *The Armies of the Night*, "Ten Thousand Words a Minute" can afford such extravagance because the man who speculates so largely is himself the object of dramatic irony. Mailer is revealed here in a familiar role: "Once more I had tried to become a hero, and had ended as an eccentric" (*TPP*, 265). Yet the speculations offered above are not to be dismissed as quirkish lunacies. As in his later works, Mailer wins a hearing for his insights as constituting the best fruit of a writer who will reveal everything about himself—his most ridiculous "capers" as well as his most dazzling intellectual connections.

The essay's final sections make it clear that Mailer's ultimate subject is himself. Once he has described the fight and offered his ideas as to what it all "meant" (i.e., what the fighters represented), Mailer's job would appear to be done. Yet he goes on for another fifteen pages. The fight inspires a severe self-analysis in which Mailer takes upon himself part of the blame for Patterson's defeat. (Briefly, Mailer finds that he has backed Patterson in an "idle, detached fashion"; like Patterson's liberal supporters, he has failed to nourish the champion's spirit—*TPP*, 258.) Here Mailer, considering events of that week in Chicago, including his debate with William Buckley at Medinah Temple, finds that the ledgers are stacked heavily against him. He has supported Patterson too complacently, he has drunk much too much, he has sulked over such trivialities as the account of his debate in the *New York Times*. Mailer feels something like Patterson's humiliation because he has identified with the lonely artist in Patterson:

Patterson was the champion of every lonely adolescent and every man who had been forced to live alone, every protagonist who tried to remain unique in a world whose waters washed apathy and compromise into the pores. He was the hero of all those unsung romantics who walk the street at night seeing the vision of Napoleon while their feet trip over the curb, he was part of the fortitude which could sustain those who lived for principle, those who had gone to war with themselves and ended with discipline (*TPP*, 241-42).

Mailer has failed both Patterson and himself, for his week in Chicago has been ruled by the world's apathy, compromise, and lack of discipline.

His disruption of Liston's press conference, the essay's final episode, reveals Mailer as yet another unsung romantic who has a vision of being Napoleon while tripping over a curb. The scene is saved from bathos, however, because Mailer sees it for what it is ("Once more I had tried to become a hero, and had ended as an eccentric"). Yet it is also a fitting climax to his narrative, for here Mailer dramatizes his determination to be "some sort of center about which all that had been lost must now rally" (*TPP*, 261). The defeat of Patterson has become for Mailer the defeat of love and art and discipline. His bravura at the press conference registers his decision to reaffirm all that the week's events and the fight itself have called into question. Indeed, this reaffirmation is what the essay is ultimately "about." By intimately describing his reactions to the fighters, Mailer has made us see that Patterson and Liston do not merely represent such forces as love and sex; they finally represent *us*, allowing us to identify with a heroic—or demonic——part of ourselves. Mailer has come to *see* this identification and to act according to its dictates—however "comic" his action may be. We, his readers, are hard put to find fault with him.

Years later Mailer would involve himself in another struggle where the opposing sides would suggest the "countered halves" of his own nature (*TPP*, 261). In his account of the 1967 March on the Pentagon, Mailer would again dramatize his conversion to one side in the struggle. Both "Ten Thousand Words a Minute" and *The Armies of the Night* are narratives about the comical yet serious education of Norman Mailer. The essay anticipates the later work in technique as well as form, for "Ten Thousand Words a Minute" depends on fictional techniques to a degree unparalleled in Mailer until *Armies*. Such devices are used selectively in "Superman Comes to the Supermarket," "In The Red Light," and "An Evening with Jackie Kennedy"; and Mailer's use of himself as a persona can be seen emerging as long ago as *Advertisements for Myself*, where his controversial self-portrait is a major unifying device. But in "Ten Thousand Words a Minute" Mailer's fictionlike nonfiction is fully developed. Such figures as Patterson, Liston, D'Amato, Jacobs, and the cabbie who takes Mailer to Comiskey Park are treated in a manner Mailer formerly reserved for his fiction. Mailer dramatizes every scene in the essay and makes particular use of the flashback, a device normally associated with fiction. If he is to be seen here as "hobbled to the facts of time, place, self," Mailer is also to be seen deploying his "facts" in a literary structure which anticipates the subjective history of *The Armies of the Night*.

The most "novelistic" of his essays, "Ten Thousand Words a Minute" is also the piece in which Mailer's self-reference is most conspicuous. For this reason, it is not surprising that the essay has received insufficient recognition as a minor masterpiece. Nor is it really curious that Mailer's nonfiction should be so seldom examined. As Scott Fitzgerald once remarked, "There are always those to whom all self-revelation is contemptible, unless it ends with a noble thanks to the gods for the Unconquerable Soul."[17] Mailer's detractors have been quick to find *his* self-revelations contemptible, failing to see that in registering its effects upon himself Mailer has illuminated the history of his time. He has offered his reactions to modern life as those of a representative American—unusually sensitive and intelligent, perhaps, but subject to the same contradictory emotions as the rest of us in confronting such phenomena as Goldwater, Floyd Patterson, the peace movement, Women's Liberation, the space program, and such enigmas as Richard Milhous Nixon. As Mailer says, there is no history without nuance. What his method suggests is that the nuances of recent history can only be caught in the response of a troubled American to those events which *are* America. If he has shown this most convincingly in *The Armies of the Night*, Mailer has anticipated that achievement in the essays I have grouped here as constituting a fourth and most appealing Mailer miscellany.

The Armies of the Night: *The Education of Norman Mailer*

MAILER once remarked that with the stabbing of his second wife he lost all chance of becoming an American Jeremiah.[1] Nothing else he has ever said about his ambitions as a writer is as revealing. Of course, there is something a bit comical in the suggestion that Mailer's talents recall Jeremiah, but those of us who sympathize with his work will perhaps forgive the hyperbole. However pretentious, Mailer's remark hints at his deeply felt desire to be something more than a respected literary figure. In 1959 Mailer announced his modest goal of creating "a revolution in the consciousness of our time" (*Adv*, 17). If he has had nothing resembling such an impact, he has persisted in his belief that the great writer and the great prophet should merge in a single figure (one who resembles Norman Mailer).

Mailer's prophetic inclinations have shaped most of his works since *Advertisments for Myself*. Increasingly suspicious of the novel's immediate "relevance," Mailer has devoted more and more of his time to nonfiction, where he could suggest not only the sources of that "plague" he sees everywhere in the land but also its possible remedies. Thus we have been offered what sometimes seems an endless supply of Mailer nonfiction, beginning with his political essays of the early 1960s and highlighted by his analysis of American social currents in *The Armies of the Night* and *Miami and the Siege of Chicago*. Though he has lavished the accumulated lore of a novelist on these works, Mailer's final purpose has been consistent with the connotations of "analysis." What he would do is tell us something about America, about ourselves. Mailer once referred to himself as "a poor man's version of Orson Welles" (*Armies*, p. 32),[2] but his real ambition has been to offer a modest version of the prophet himself.

Mailer has come closest to this ideal in *The Armies of the Night* (1968), a book which climaxes his decade-long concern with "the task of examining America" (*CC*, 99). This achievement is at once the culmination of much earlier work and the luckiest of accidents. Technically, *Armies* draws upon Mailer's work in nonfiction throughout the 1960s, as I suggested in chapter five. But if it now seems the "inevitable" climax to this earlier work, such a book was far from Mailer's mind when he was first invited to attend the 1967 March on the Pentagon. Whereas Truman Capote went looking for a "true" event worthy of being immortalized in a "nonfiction novel," Mailer came into his materials rather against his will. Mailer's reluctance even to attend the demonstration is great irony today, for by the end of that eventful weekend in Washington he knew that he had stumbled upon a literary treasure. The march proved once more what Mailer had been saying for years, that in the twentieth century "the real had become more fantastic than the imagined."[3] The march was precisely Mailer's kind of material, for as he once said, "mate the absurd with the apocalyptic, and I was a captive" (*Adv*, 221). The absurd, the apocalyptic, and Mailer came together that October weekend in Washington, and a book was born. What began as a wasted weekend participating in "idiot mass manifestations" (18) ended by inspiring Mailer's most successful work.

This opinion is surprisingly widespread. *Armies* received almost uniformly excellent reviews and won both the Pulitzer Prize and the National Book Award. Today one doesn't have to defend the quality of this book (as one must defend the quality of *The Deer Park*, for example). Yet for all its good reviews and awards, *Armies* raises certain questions which its critics have tended to ignore. They have acknowledged its essential wisdom, the chastened prophetic strain which here informs the work of a man who once said he wanted to create a revolution in the consciousness of our time. But Mailer's critics have been all too timid in discussing the narrative strategy by which he channels his prophetic desires into meaningful form. Those who acclaim Mailer's "objective" self-portrait have ignored the narrative pattern he imposes on his work by means of this portrait. Those who refer to Mailer's formal "breakthrough" have dealt with the book's initial, "novelistic" section as if it were formally unrelated to the second, "historical" part. Surely these are important matters. What *is* the narrative pattern in *Armies*? Is it a "nonfiction novel" or is it a history? Indeed, is it fiction or nonfiction? If we cannot answer questions of this sort, we are in no position to praise *Armies* as Mailer's masterpiece. And if *Armies* is a work of real distinction—if it

is more than a "report" on Mailer's role in a peace demonstration—
then surely something must be made of its apparently independent
parts. Mailer came to write book two of *Armies* after having fulfilled
his obligation to *Harper's* by writing book one. It would be well for his
literary reputation, therefore, if he had something in mind other than
padding out his account of the march to the dimensions of a
full-length book.[4]

In what follows, then, I want to do three things: discuss the generic
question which *Armies* raises, describe the narrative pattern of book
one, and suggest how the two halves of *Armies* are related. By
clarifying its structure, I hope to show that *Armies* is a powerful
synthesis of Mailer's artistic and prophetic ambitions.

I   *The Generic Question*

"History as a Novel/The Novel as History"—Mailer's subtitle calls
attention to one of the more obvious questions about *Armies*. What
kind of animal is this book, a history or a novel? Because we bring
such very different expectations to works of fiction and nonfiction, I
assume this question is not irrelevant, as some have argued. Before
discussing the book's form, however, I want to comment on two other
American works which have challenged the traditional distinction
between fiction and nonfiction. If we compare these books with
Armies, I think we can better understand Mailer's formal innovations. I have in mind Hemingway's *Green Hills of Africa* and Capote's
In Cold Blood. Like Mailer, Hemingway and Capote not only employ
some of the devices of fiction in the service of nonfiction; they
presume to employ *all* (or nearly all) fictional devices in the creation
of what Capote has called the "nonfiction novel."

This is not quite the claim that Hemingway makes for *Green Hills
of Africa* (1935). In his foreword to this work, Hemingway in fact
draws attention to the *difference* between his book and "many
novels": "Unlike many novels, none of the characters or incidents in
this book is imaginary. . . . The writer has attempted to write an
absolutely true book to see whether the shape of a country and the
pattern of a month's action can, if truly presented, compete with a
work of the imagination." *Green Hills of Africa* is, therefore, a pure
example of nonfiction: "an absolutely true book." Yet the work reads
much like a novel. Hemingway dramatizes his material as he would in
a work of fiction, even to the point of altering the chronology of events
to achieve such "fictional" effects as suspense and a narrative climax.[5]

The usual defense for material included in a work of nonfiction—things happened this way—doesn't altogether apply to Hemingway's book. So "novelistic" does it seem, the literary conversations at the beginning impress us as digressive; quite simply, they detract from the story which is developed everywhere else in the book. These conversations may have occurred just as Hemingway describes them, yet they have no meaningful relation to anything else in the work. This seems suggestive, for if we begin to evaluate a book by its internal coherence and not its fidelity to fact, shouldn't we also conclude that it is structured as fiction rather than nonfiction? If we *seem* to be reading a novel, isn't it the case that we *are* reading a novel (one that happens to be "absolutely true")?

But how unfortunate for Hemingway's reputation if we decide that *Green Hills of Africa* is a novel. Artfully structured to achieve a dramatic climax in its hero's hunt for kudu, *Green Hills of Africa* is nonetheless a powderpuff of a novel. More to the point, it isn't a novel at all. We see this most clearly in the book's principal characterization. "Hemingway" is the work's protagonist, yet he is entirely without depth as a character. We learn nothing about him when he finally gets his kudu hunt, nor have we learned much earlier except that he is persistent and loves to hunt. In point of fact, "Hemingway" is a device which allows Hemingway to work up his real—and announced—concerns: "the shape of a country and the pattern of a month's action." We learn almost nothing about "Hemingway's" past, not because Hemingway has chosen to develop his hero in terms of the present, but because he is committed to describing one month's activities on safari in Africa. To go into "Hemingway's" past would only distract us from the work's fundamental concerns—concerns which are documentary and not novelistic, nonfictional and not imaginary. *Green Hills of Africa* is a marvelous account of hunting in Africa. We do Hemingway no favor by insisting that it is a novel about a man named "Hemingway" who achieves the hunt of his life after many frustrations.

Truman Capote also wanted to produce "an absolutely true book" when he came to write *In Cold Blood* (1965). Capote has gone so far as to argue that *everything* in his book is "immaculately factual": "One doesn't spend almost six years on a book, the point of which is factual accuracy, and then give way to minor distractions."[6] Capote presses this claim both in his subtitle ("A True Account of a Multiple Murder and Its Consequences") and in his acknowledgments: "All the material in this book not derived from my own observations is either taken from official records or is the result of interviews with the persons directly concerned, more often than not numerous interviews conducted over a considerable period of time." Since we *expect* a work of nonfiction to be accurate, Capote's remarks are interesting only because he has also insisted that his book is formally unique, a "nonfiction novel."

Capote has defined the nonfiction novel as "a narrative form that employ[s] all the techniques of fictional art but [is] nevertheless immaculately factual."[7] Readers who believe that Capote has achieved this form have naturally emphasized the novelistic character of *In Cold Blood*. David Galloway, for example, has praised Capote for "a careful and artful selection of details, calculated to evoke a variety of moods, to establish character, to produce suspense, and to convey a number of intricately related themes. It is in the selection of such details and in their rearrangement that the technique of the novelist is vividly present . . ."[8] But does novelistic technique inevitably point to the form of the novel? This would appear to be the crucial question—one neither Capote nor his partisans have directly addressed. It seems to me that what Capote has done hardly differs from what Hemingway wished to do in *Green Hills of Africa*. When Capote remarked that the "point" of his book was its factual accuracy, he defined it as that most stolid form of historical writing, a documentary.

The novelist is free to depict only the most "authentic" persons, places, and things; like the "naturalists," he may insist that his fictional world is "life-like," a genuine representation of the world we all know and move about in. Every detail in his book may in fact be "true." For example, Henry Miller may well have rendered his experiences more accurately than either Hemingway or Capote.[9] But it really doesn't matter whether Miller is as "accurate" or not. Because he doesn't *claim* that his books are immaculately factual— because he offers them as novels—we in fact read them as fictions, never thinking to condemn their author if we should find that he has "distorted" events of his own life. I think we would condemn Hemingway or Capote if we found that either had seriously distorted the truth.[10]

I am suggesting that from the moment we first read Capote's subtitle we begin to assimilate his material as the evidence in his reconstruction of a true event. We don't ask of this evidence that it be "probable" or arranged in some effective, climactic fashion. If it is so arranged, we receive a more powerful impression of the evidence without ceasing to evaluate it as such—we do not cease to read the book as a documentary. Of course, this would not remain the case if *In Cold Blood* differed from a book like *Tropic of Cancer* only in the claim which appears on its title page. But it happens that this claim is more or less accurate. We continue to read *In Cold Blood* as a documentary because finally it *is* a documentary. The resemblance to fictional structure in Capote's book is really quite superficial. As Capote tells us, his materials have been selected because they *are* the Clutter murder case in all its solid specificity. Capote has rearranged a few events, but this rearrangment should not be confused with the imaginative structure of a fiction. Unlike the novelist, Capote cannot alter the events or details of his story in order to develop character or theme; indeed, he can do nothing which might violate the factual accuracy of his account. The inevitable result is that character and theme, as we know them in the novel, simply do not appear in a book like *In Cold Blood*. This is suggested by the fact that Capote's central characters have no more depth than Hemingway's persona. We could argue that Capote has simply failed as a nonfiction novelist, but I think the explanation is otherwise. I don't think it accidental that "Henry Miller," as revealed in Miller's novels, is a much richer creation than anyone in Capote's book. The events in these novels may be "real," but they have been introduced because they dramatize the many sides of Miller's controversial hero. After all, the revelation of character is what Miller—as novelist—is principally about. The writer who would document an event may well find that to "develop" his characters actually runs counter to his basic intention. I believe this is true for Hemingway and Capote in the works I have been discussing.

These remarks on Hemingway and Capote may seem somewhat gratuitous, but I hope to demonstrate their relevance to what Mailer has done in *Armies*. The comparison suggests itself because *Armies* shares so many features with *Green Hills of Africa* and *In Cold Blood*. Like these books, *Armies* is an experiment in nonfiction by a famous writer who brings to his task the accumulated resources of a novelist. Like Hemingway, Mailer uses himself as the protagonist of his book. Like Capote, Mailer selects a subject which offers what David Galloway has called "instant symbolism," a subject which embodies his longstanding thematic concerns. Tony Tanner has summed up what is symbolically apposite about Capote's material: "By juxtaposing and dovetailing the lives and values of the Clutters and those of the killers, Capote produces a stark image of the deep doubleness of

American life."[11] Mailer also believes in this deep doubleness—as Tanner acknowledges by citing the passage in "Superman Comes to the Supermaket" where Mailer speaks of America's "double life" (*TPP*, 38). In *Armies*, Mailer finds yet another image of America's deep doubleness in the forces which confront each other during the March on the Pentagon. These armies of our divided country seem almost to have been magically invoked for Mailer's purposes.

Mailer's narrative techniques also recall Hemingway and Capote. Most obviously there is the full-scale use of novelistic devices, especially techniques of dramatization such as Mailer calls attention to with his subtitle. Like Capote, however, Mailer also relies on public sources in rendering his story. These sources allow him to cover events he did not personally witness.[12] Mailer also follows Capote in digressing from his narrative to analyze issues relevant to the event he is describing. Where Capote presents a psychoanalytic interpretation of Perry Smith, one of his two mass-murderers (*In Cold Blood*, pp. 328-39), Mailer offers an argument on why we are in Vietnam and why we should get out (181-89). The resulting blend of novelistic and nonfictional devices extends the method Mailer first developed in the shorter form of the personal essay. Capote went through a similar training for *In Cold Blood* with interviews he published in *The New Yorker* and in his book *The Muses are Heard*.[13]

Is *Armies* a history, then? Like *Green Hills of Africa*, does it try to capture a real event with absolute truth? Like *In Cold Blood*, is its principle of selection factual accuracy? Or does *Armies* differ significantly from these two works? I believe that it does differ, though not as fiction differs from journalism. I think we must finally read *Armies* as a history and not as a novel; but we must also see that it is a very unusual history, quite different from what Hemingway and Capote have created.

Mailer's subtitle hardly makes it clear that *Armies* is a history, but in the work itself there is abundant evidence that he conceived his book in this way. At the end of part I (book one), Mailer sends his protagonist home from the Ambassador Theatre to his room at the Hay-Adams Hotel. He then remarks, "Of course if this were a novel, Mailer would spend the rest of the night with a lady. But it is history, and so the Novelist is for once blissfully removed from any description of the hump-your-backs of sex" (52). Later, following his release from jail, Mailer says that "then he began his history of the Pentagon." He characterizes this work as "history in the costume of a novel" (215). Besides these passing references to *Armies* as a history,

Mailer offers a defense of his narrative method which clearly shows that *Armies* is a history (albeit a special version of history, closely related to the novel).

Mailer defends his method early in book one. Here he explains why it is proper for him "to write an intimate history of an event which places its focus on a central figure who is not central to the event"—that is, himself. This procedure is justified by the nature of the March on the Pentagon, "an ambiguous event whose essential value or absurdity may not be established for ten or twenty years, or indeed ever." Mailer argues that to focus on one of the founders or designers of the march—David Dellinger, Jerry Rubin, *et al.*—would resolve none of the ambiguity. For this we need "an eyewitness who is a participant but not a vested partisan . . . ambiguous in his own proportions, a comic hero." Given such a hero, Mailer hopes "to recapture the precise feel of the ambiguity of the event and its monumental disproportions" (53).

Mailer's defense of his method may or may not seem plausible. In any case, it does define his major objective in *Armies*: "to recapture the precise feel of the ambiguity of the event." This may be compared to what Hemingway attempted in *Green Hills of Africa*, where Hemingway used himself as a vehicle to suggest what it was like to hunt in Africa. Both Mailer and Hemingway are primarily interested in the *event* they describe—an historian's interest, not a novelist's. Yet Mailer's definition is interesting, for it almost outlines the intentions of a novelist. To recapture the precise *feel* of an event is to search for nuance instead of fact, ever Mailer's intention in his nonfiction; and to recapture what an event *feels* like requires that he create a protagonist who can register this feeling in himself and in others. Writing his history of the march, Mailer ends by developing his own character much as he would a fictional hero's.

Throughout his nonfiction Mailer has presented himself as such a persona. In *Miami and the Siege of Chicago*, he suggests the reason for this: "If this were essentially an account of the reporter's actions, it would be interesting to follow him through the chutes on Thursday, but we are concerned with his actions only as they illumine the event of the Republican Convention in Miami, the Democratic Convention in Chicago, and the war of the near streets" (p. 197). In *Armies*, too, Mailer uses himself as a means toward illuminating the event he is describing. But in *Armies* Mailer illumines the event by describing *all* of his actions during the march. The difference is quantitative, but as Mailer is fond of saying (quoting Engels), quantity affects quality.

Formally, *The Armies of the Night* is closely related to *Miami and the Siege of Chicago* (as well as to the essays discussed in chapter five). Yet it is different, too, for Mailer has employed his method so exhaustively as to create a form almost indistinguishable from the novel.

He has done this for the reason offered in the text: that in order to understand the March on the Pentagon, we must understand its essential ambiguity, the *feel* of its ambiguity. We must grasp its "subjective reality." This is the phrase Tom Wolfe uses to describe what he is after in *The Electric Kool-Aid Acid Test* (1969), yet another book sometimes referred to as a nonfiction novel. In an "author's note," Wolfe says that he has tried "not only to tell what the Pranksters did but to recreate the mental atmosphere or subjective reality of it." What Wolfe says of his book about Ken Kesey and the Merry Pranksters, Mailer might have said about *Armies*. But Mailer would never have gone on to say, as Wolfe does, that "all the events, details, and dialogue I have recorded are either what I saw and heard myself or were told to me by people who were there themselves or were recorded on tapes or film or in writing."[14] For from here it is but a short step to Capote's explicit claim: this work is to be judged by how accurate it is. To say the least, Mailer has small sympathy for such claims to "accuracy." At the end of *Armies*, he writes of events at the Pentagon after the massive crowds have departed and the few remaining demonstrators are left alone with the soldiers. He first reprints two remarkably dissimilar accounts of what happened at this time (260-62), then comments, "It may be obvious by now that a history of the March on the Pentagon which is not unfair will never be written, any more than a history which could prove dependable in details!" (262). Mailer is indeed writing history in *Armies*, but it is a very subjective history; and the difference between subjective history and fiction is a subject on which most theorists fear to tread.

Treading softly, I would suggest at least two differences between these forms. The first is fairly obvious. Any history, no matter how subjective, is based on fact as a fiction is not. This may seem to contradict what I have just said about Mailer's attitude toward "accuracy," but the contradiction is more apparent than real. The subjective historian does not claim to be absolutely accurate in reporting "what happened"; indeed, his concern is to *interpret* what happened, to discover its real significance. Nonetheless, he acknowledges that his work is founded on what actually occurred. Mailer acknowledges this throughout *Armies*, as when he remarks that he isn't obliged to work up a love interest for all us novel-readers. He isn't obliged to do this because his narrative is restricted to what happened during four days in October, 1967. Fortunately, what happened to Mailer is interesting (if sexless) material. Yet the "rightness" of his material doesn't alter the fact that by his choice of forms Mailer has denied himself the enriching possibilities of imaginary episodes.

A second difference between subjective history and fiction is rather more important. These forms differ in their basic ends. As I have suggested, the historian wishes to discover the meaning of the event which is his subject. If his method is subjective, he may render his own impressions of the event, or the impressions of others; he may even dramatize the entire event as he experienced it. But he will do so for the reason Mailer offers in the passage quoted above: to illumine the event itself. Most fictions are structured toward a very different end. I take this end to be the creation of emotional effects—tragic, comic, etc.—appropriate to the particular fictional action. The characters in a fiction exist for the sake of such effects, then, and not to "explain" an external phenomenon (the March on the Pentagon, say).[15] Another way of putting this is that Mailer's personal story is developed so that we may finally understand the March on the Pentagon, while the fictitious Huck Finn's story is presented for its own sake. In this context, the crucial fact about *Armies* is that it doesn't end with book one as a novel on the same subject might have. Book two is relevant precisely *because Armies* is a history, i.e., because its formal end is to interpret an historical event rather than dramatize its hero's spiritual growth. Book two extends Mailer's avowed purpose, "to elucidate the mysterious character of that quintessentially American event [the March on the Pentagon]" (216). As we sense well before Mailer explains its purpose, book one prepares for book two. Mailer's historical intentions, advertised throughout, lead us to expect that his highly personal account of the march will issue finally in a subjective but general interpretation of the event as a whole. When this in fact occurs in book two, we should realize that *Armies* is not organized as a novel.

The temptation to read *Armies* as a novel is not the real danger to its reputation, however. The real danger is that *Armies* will be considered a documentary. If it is right to see that *Armies* is not a novel, it is even more important that we appreciate how it differs from books like *Green Hills of Africa* and *In Cold Blood*. The difference lies principally in Mailer's treatment of his own character. Hemingway directs our attention to his African setting and the events of his hunt by refusing to develop himself as a "rounded" character; Capote rigorously excludes from the account his own role in the Clutter investigation to concentrate on the data he has accumulated. Mailer emphasizes instead his own reactions to the March on the Pentagon. These internal "events" are hardly verifiable in the manner of a documentary. In no meaningful way could it be argued that Mailer has "documented" his response to the march. Rather, he has used his reactions as the material for what he calls his "interior" history of the demonstration (255).

These distinctions may seem a bit academic, but they have the value of suggesting that book two of *Armies* is an integral part of Mailer's work. Before we can appreciate this, however, we must first understand what Mailer has done in book one. What distinguishes book one is that Mailer has fulfilled his obligations as historian while writing a narrative which also has the appeal of a novel. Whether or not his material is inherently interesting, Mailer has made it seem so by means of the novelistic "costume" in which he has clothed it. As I suggested earlier, the shape of this costume has not been much discussed. In a sense, of course, Mailer's form was imposed on him by his choice of the historical mode. But however "factual," the form of book one is not merely chronological. The events form a narrative pattern—a plot—which though rooted in "what happened" is much more significant. There is a meaning to the events which Mailer is able to get at *because* his history is subjective. To see how this is so, we must first turn to Mailer's portrait of Mailer.

II   *The Structure of Book One*

"From the outset, let us bring you news of your protagonist" (3). In this, the first sentence in *Armies*, Mailer introduces his hero. He will refer to him later as the Participant, the Historian, the Novelist, and the Existentialist. He will refer to him as "a simple of a hero" (215). Readers who come to Mailer's book by way of his legend as a self-advertising egomaniac must be puzzled to learn that Mailer is here laughing at Norman Mailer.

Mailer's decision to write about himself in the third person is oddly reminiscent of *The Education of Henry Adams*. While a full-scale comparison of *Armies* and the *Education* would be absurd,[16] the similarities are interesting. D. W. Brogan has summarized the *Education* in this fashion: "It is indeed, on the surface, the story of one who failed because, trained to be at home in Franklin's world, he had to live in a world transformed by the new science and the new technology."[17] Mailer's readers will recall *his* obsession with the evils of technology, his increasing conservatism as he confronts the modern technocracy. In much of his writing (*Cannibals and Christians*, say), Mailer rivals Adams as a pessimistic analyst of the machine age. In *Armies*, Mailer's Pentagon is as much a symbol for this age as the dynamo was for Adams. I don't want to push this comparison too far—Henry Adams and Norman Mailer will not seem every reader's idea of soul-brothers—but the likeness does suggest Mailer's increasingly conservative image of himself, rendered most fully in *Armies*. It also suggests the seeming objectivity of this image, achieved partly by use of the distancing third person, partly by an exceedingly scrupulous—and Adams-like—inquiry into the author's personality.

Mailer's baroque personality is the figure in the carpet so far as *Armies* is concerned; and this personality *is* baroque—as baroque as Mailer's description of it: "Now Mailer was often brusque himself, famous for that, but the architecture of his personality bore resemblance to some provincial cathedral which warring orders of the church might have designed separately over several centuries, the particular cathedral falling into the hands of one architect, then his enemy. (Mailer had not been married four times for nothing.)" (17) Indeed, Mailer is fairly merciless in pointing up his own mistakes and unworthy feelings. He tries always to view himself as others do, no matter how unflattering the result. He can admit that he is "much too vain" to wear eyeglasses before professional photographers (106); he can acknowledge the "hot anger" he feels because Robert Lowell is loved and he is not (45); he can note his desire for a hasty arrest at the Pentagon in order to return to New York for a dinner party (118-19); he can characterize some of his actions in jail as those of a "mountebank" (173).

Yet our comic hero is not so much unlikable as he is contradictory. He is a "notable," a famous writer worthy of being petitioned to lend his name to the antiwar demonstrations; yet he is capable of beliefs like the following: "He had the idea—it was undeniably oversimple—that if you spent too much time on the phone in the evening, you destroyed some kind of creativity for the dawn" (4). He is "a snob of the worst sort" (14) and captive to a "wild man" in himself, referred to rather tolerantly as "the Beast" (30); yet he is a loving, even sentimental, husband and father (166-71); he is even a patriot of the first rank (47, 113). Once dedicated to revolutionary socialism, he is at heart a *grand conservateur* (18). Mailer's many contradictions are best illustrated by his confessed ideological position as a "Left Conservative" (124). During his mayoral campaign of 1969, Mailer was fond of saying that he was running further to the left and further to the right than any of the other candidates. In *Armies,* too, Mailer can be seen running in many directions at once.

But in book one Mailer does not randomly expose the many fine and ugly features of his character. Book one traces an extremely important moment in the history of this complex personality when Mailer's divided self achieved at least temporary wholeness during the March on the Pentagon. Later, we will see that this account is crucial to Mailer's interpretation of the march. For the moment, it is enough to remark that the structure of book one corresponds to the stages of Mailer's spiritual experience.

Mailer's less endearing features are naturally emphasized early in book one where we encounter that side of his personality which is to be transcended in the course of the march. Here we are introduced to Mailer's theory of evening telephone calls, his "virtual" conservatism on the subject of drugs (5) and his "neo-Victorianism" on the subject of sex (24). Here we observe his very reluctant acceptance of Mitchell Goodman's invitation to attend the antiwar demonstrations in Washington. Our hero is not very heroic in his first appearance. He is depicted as more concerned about editing his latest movie and attending his Saturday night dinner engagement than with actively protesting the war in Vietnam. Indeed, he looks forward to his weekend of "idiot mass manifestations" as in every way a lost weekend: "Mailer wished as the Washington weekend approached that the Washington weekend were done" (10). Mailer's portrait of himself as a touchy and incongruous "revolutionary-for-a-weekend" (56) is confirmed by his distaste for the "innocent" young girls and liberal academics who surround him at the buffet he attends his first night in Washington (13-16). His masterless performance as master of ceremonies at the ensuing rally climaxes the portrayal of our much flawed hero on the eve of the demonstrations (28-52).

But if Mailer begins *Armies* by revealing the more comical aspects of his own character, he does so in full confidence that book one as a whole will place them in an artful and not unappealing perspective. In fact, the rest of book one records Mailer's conversion to the cause he has ostensibly come to Washington to support. Part II of book one depicts his shift from apathy to involvement, as Mailer is variously impressed by a number of demonstrators who do not conform to his stereotype of the ineffectual "liberal academic": students representing different chapters of Resist, an antiwar organization (61-63); William Sloane Coffin, Jr., Chaplain at Yale (66-67); Robert Lowell, when this poet addresses the demonstrators at the Department of Justice. Lowell has figured prominently in the events of part I, where Mailer offers a chilly account of Lowell's motives and general character. Now Mailer concedes that "all flaws considered, Lowell was still a fine, good, and honorable man, and Norman Mailer was happy to be linked in a cause with him" (74). Unmistakably, as this first day of protest nears its end, Mailer has begun to join the "cause" himself. He even speaks to the demonstrators, advising that perhaps the time had come "when Americans, many Americans, would have to face the possibility of going to jail for their ideas" (79). It is after this speech, after this day of antiwar activities, that Mailer first commits himself to staying for the March on the Pentagon.

As Saturday arrives (part III), it is clear that Mailer has assimilated Friday's lessons. No longer does he think of the protest as "idiot mass manifestations." Now as later he believes that the march is "that first major battle of a war which may go on for twenty years"; he even entertains the idea "that in fifty years the day may loom in our history as large as the ghosts of the Union dead" (88). Mailer is all but liberated by the prospect of leading his newly discovered "troops," the hippies and other young people who are a majority of the demonstrators (he is to be their general, of course). Assured that he is engaged in a noble work and capable of performing his part without fear (113), subsequently "lifted" into a sense of "comradeship" by the tribalistic music of the Fugs (125), Mailer gives himself up to the spirit of the protest by "transgressing" a police line and getting arrested (129-31). The act isn't obviously heroic, yet it does issue from Mailer's new sense of commitment and comradeship, the growth of which he has traced throughout book one. Therefore he can describe this act—with saving humor—as "his Rubicon" (138).

During part III Mailer has not portrayed his hero as altogether transfigured. The great Mailer ego remains on display, as when he decides on a quick arrest in order to obtain a quick release ("Such men are either monumental fools or excruciatingly practical"—p. 119). References to one's Rubicon do not signal absolute humility. But reminders of Mailer's none too flawless personality only emphasize by contrast the remarkable conversion he in fact undergoes. They take the curse off his account of how he got religion in the country of the young and the liberal academic.

It is hardly a metaphor to say that Mailer "gets religion" during the march. For Mailer, the experience is nothing less than a rite of purification. At the Lincoln Memorial, he decides to observe a fast until the march is over (106). This hint of a purification ritual is reinforced once he is arrested. Mailer notes that "he felt as if he were being confirmed" by his arrest (138); later, he says that "he felt shriven" (158). Throughout his stay in jail Mailer feels an exaltation we normally associate with saintliness (even in saints so unlikely as Mailer): ". . . and he knew by the unfamiliar variety of happiness he now felt that much indeed had happened to him" (160). He breaks his fast only when assured that he has passed his "test": "He had felt, despite every petty motive, or low calculation on how to get back to New York for the party, a mild exaltation on which he had traveled through the day, a sense of cohering in himself which was he supposed the opposite of those more familiar states of alienation he could always describe so well" (162-63). When released on Sunday morning, Mailer is sure that his experience has been liberating: ". . . he felt one suspicion of a whole man closer to that freedom from dread which occupied the inner drama of his years, yes, one image closer than when he had come to Washington four days ago" (212-13).

Book one dramatizes this change in Mailer. It describes an experience almost religious in nature. This conviction lies behind Mailer's otherwise curious remarks upon leaving the makeshift courtroom at Occoquan, Virginia. Here Mailer says that protests like the march may have to become more militant because " 'we are burning the body and blood of Christ in Vietnam. Yes, we are burning him there, and as we do, we destroy the foundation of this Republic, which is its love and trust in Christ' " (214). Behind his statement rests Mailer's conception of America as a Christian country. For Mailer, Christianity is marked by its belief in mysteries, the greatest of which is "the bleeding heart of Christ." Vietnam reveals that America has lost its soul to "a worship of technology," for Vietnam is *the* technological war (188). Mystery ("the bleeding heart of Christ") has been replaced by the procedures of technology; therefore, by implication, we are burning the body and blood of Christ in Vietnam.

Mailer's statement issues from the dramatic context not only of his release from prison but also the completion of a liberating, quasireligious experience begun in apathy but ended in "mild exaltation." It derives from a mind spiritually refreshed and inclined toward the solemnity of things religious. We will encounter this mind again, at the end of book two, where Mailer will speak not of his own experience but the general experience of the demonstrators. In tracing his own belated conversion, Mailer therefore prepares for the more general rite of passage which is to be celebrated in book two. What appears to be an egotistical emphasis on his own actions is really Mailer's attempt to persuade us that his reactions are representative. We see as he sees; we share his initial indifference to this "radical" act of civil disobedience; then, if we are in fact persuaded, we experience with him the transforming event the march ultimately became; and having passed through this experience with Mailer, we are prepared for his retrospective analysis of the march which follows in book two.

III   *The Relevance of Book Two*

That is one answer, of course, to the question of how Mailer's personal story is relevant to the materials of book two. At the beginning of book two, Mailer takes up this question himself. Here he tells us that book one is to be "a tower fully equipped with telescopes to study—at the greatest advantage—our own horizon" (219). He makes it clear that *Armies* should not be read as a novel, for the "novel" of book one is a means toward an end. Book one—our metaphorical tower—is to provide the perspective we need on the massive and somewhat chaotic particulars of the march itself. It does so in at least three ways: it offers intimate portraits of the various political factions involved in the march—left, right, and center; it establishes Mailer's right to speak of the march in the impersonal, authoritative tone of book two, since it bears witness to his profound involvement in the event ("I suffered, I was there"); and it provides, in Mailer's transformation from comic hero to mildly exalted initiate, a model for the experience of the demonstrators, who will be shown undergoing an analogous experience from the initial, humorous negotiations for the march to the final, transfiguring events of Saturday night at the Pentagon.

Book two returns to the beginning to trace the genesis and execution of the march. "Obedient to a general style of historical writing" (255), book two is a history of the march which focuses on its major figures, the antiwar leaders and their counterparts in the government, the students and soldiers who confront each other at the Pentagon. In 1963 Mailer could write, "The play of political ideas is flaccid here in America because opposing armies never meet. The Right, the Center, and what there is of the Left have set up encampments on separate hills . . . No Man's Land predominates. It is a situation which calls for guerrilla raiders" (*TPP*, 25). Book two documents the emergence of such guerrillas. It is a history of opposing armies very much in conflict.

Of course, Mailer has depicted these "armies" throughout book one. His portraits there both illustrate and occasion his analysis of America—always the final end in Mailer's fictionlike nonfiction. Chapter two of part IV offers, in the marshal and the nazi, prototypes of that cannibalistic rightwing Mailer has described so well in his account of the 1964 Republican convention, "In The Red Light." Latter-day versions of the Wasp, these men suggest to Mailer the bigotry his own "army" must transform if it is to alter America. Other figures of the right described in *Armies* are more sympathetic but no less alienated from the demonstrators who have come to Washington to protest the war. In the eyes of a turnkey, for example, Mailer discovers "narrowness, propriety, good-will, and that infernal American innocence which could not question one's leaders, for madness and the boils of a frustrated life resided beneath" (169). Mailer is equally saddened by those "clean American kids" who stare at the demonstrators, for they bring home the fact that marshals and turnkeys have children who will never gather in Washington to protest American wars (156).

Mailer's attention in *Armies* is more often devoted to figures of the left. As his book makes clear, the center and the left of American politics are somewhat inharmoniously united in the peace movement. The center for Mailer is liberalism, represented by those liberal academics Mailer encounters at the buffet before the meeting at the Ambassador Theatre. Mailer feels little sympathy for these people. If they oppose the war in Vietnam, they don't oppose the technological machine behind the war—their opposition to the Johnson administration is "no more than a quarrel among engineers" (15). Mailer is temperamentally opposed to the pacifism and rationality of the liberals; they are not the guerrilla raiders he has dreamed of commanding. But then neither is the old left, the least impressive radical force in the march. For Mailer, the old left is but a step removed from the liberal technologues. The former's penchant for speeches ("The Great Left Pall") is more impressive than its disposition to act (98); like the liberals, its members are "the first real champions of technology land" (96). Much more interesting is the new left. Among the young girls and hippies and SDS provocateurs, Mailer discovers a true if ignorant army to engage America's marshals and technologues.

Mailer is not entirely charmed by his troops of the new left, however. They are too much like the young girls he meets at the buffet, "innocent, decent-spirited, merry, red-cheeked, idealistic, and utterly lobotomized away from the sense of sin" (14). Mailer's sense of sin is such that he has come full circle from his search for the apocalyptic orgasm ("The White Negro") to his present "neo-Victorianism." Not for nothing is he a left *conservative*. He can describe his troops as "middle-class cancer-pushers and drug-gutted flower children" (35); he can suggest that they are "bombed by the use of LSD as outrageously as the atoll of Eniwetok, Hiroshima, Nagasaki, and the scorched foliage of Vietnam" (93). Yet they are his troops still. Mailer is very much impressed by the young people he meets during the march, e.g., the student leaders of Resist, the young man at Occoquan who "gave Mailer a critique of the staging of his play *The Deer Park* which was about as incisive as his own. A remarkable boy" (164-65). Mailer doesn't have Charles Reich's faith in the children of flowers, but neither does he feel an alien in the country of the young.[18] He is very much taken with the political tactics of the new left. For Mailer, the new left is truly a *new* political phenomenon.

Mailer finds that the young radicals make an almost absolute contrast with their older comrades:

A generation of the American young had come along different from five previous generations of the middle class. The new generation believed in technology more than any before it, but the generation also believed in LSD, in witches, in tribal knowledge, in orgy, and revolution. It had no respect whatsoever for the unassailable logic of the next step: belief was reserved for the revelatory mystery of the happening where you did not know what was going to happen next; *that was what was good about it* (86; my italics).

We recall Mailer's words at the Ambassador Theatre, where he advised those assembled that they were up against "an existential situation," the outcome of which was uncertain. Mailer's admiration for those who embrace such a situation is obvious. Here he goes on to say, "The New Left was drawing its political aesthetic from Cuba. The revolutionary idea which the followers of Castro had induced from their experience in the hills was that you created the revolution first and learned from it, learned of what your revolution might consist and where it might go out of the intimate truth of the way it presented itself to your experience" (87). Mailer sees such an aesthetic at work in the March on the Pentagon, which is why he finally endorses it. He has always sponsored such "existential" acts, for they give the lie to static political situations and force the powers involved to reveal their true natures. Thus he once wrote that "an existential political act, the drive by Southern Negroes, led by Martin Luther King, to end segregation in restaurants in Birmingham, an act which is existential precisely because its end is unknown, has succeeded en route in discovering more of the American reality to us" (TPP, 26). Thus he applauds the guerrilla tactics of the new left, for they too reveal something of the American reality.

Unhappily, what they reveal is that "the center of America might be insane." The March on the Pentagon confirms Mailer's most pessimistic analysis of the American scene: "The country had been living with a controlled, even fiercely controlled, schizophrenia which had been deepening with the years. Perhaps the point had now been passed." Mailer defines this schizophrenia as our irreconcilable allegiance both to Christianity ("Mystery") and to technology ("the love of no Mystery whatsoever"). Because they have witnessed the effects of this condition on their elders, the young have arisen in protest (188). Our plight is therefore what it seemed to Mailer as early as 1962: a tragic impasse in which "we diverge as countrymen further and further away from one another, like a space ship broken apart in flight which now drifts mournfully in isolated orbits, satellites to each other, planets none, communication faint" (TPP, 98). The March on the Pentagon is a "symbolic battle" in which no one is killed (199), but what it symbolizes is so agonizing that it constantly reminds Mailer of the Civil War (88, 89, 91, 93, 113, 126, 263).

Mailer's purpose in *Armies* is to discover the meaning of one episode in this second Civil War. Though he is drawn to the demonstrators, his title implies that he must deal with armies equally ignorant. (The title comes, of course, from Matthew Arnold's "Dover Beach": "And we are here as on a darkling plain/ Swept with confused alarms of struggle and flight,/ Where ignorant armies clash by night.") In a sense, both armies should be seen as "villains" (93). Indeed, Mailer fears that "nihilism might be the only answer to totalitarianism" (176). Thus we see that Mailer's ignorant armies— nihilism and totalitarianism, respectively—embody very unattractive alternatives. Mailer adds that his "final allegiance" is with the villains who are hippies (93), but his reading of the embattled armies inspires no enthusiasm for his choice. If the March on the Pentagon were nothing more than a symbolic battle between unappealing forces, it would not seem to issue in anything resembling catharsis.

Yet the march does produce a catharsis. It has this effect on Mailer himself, as we have seen; and it has this effect on the "best" of the demonstrators. What Mailer charts in book two is the conversion of nihilism into purposeful rebellion, which he refers to as a rite of passage. Fittingly, it is enacted at the very end of *Armies,* where it climaxes not only the demonstration but Mailer's narrative as well.

When he comes to describe the confrontation between the sons of the middle class (the demonstrators) and the sons of the working class (the soldiers), Mailer's history of the march undergoes a definite shift in tone. The first half of book two is full of the humor of embattled armies which negotiate when and where they will confront each other, what routes the demonstrators may take and what territory they may occupy. This section of book two is therefore analogous to the first part of book one, where Mailer's misadventures are recorded similarly with an eye for the ridiculous. But just as Mailer's experience intensifies—and with it the tone of the book—so the humor of book two dissolves once Mailer turns to the events of Saturday night after the masses have departed and the most dedicated demonstrators are left alone with the soldiers. Mailer gives twenty pages to these events, among the most impressive pages he has ever written. Here we listen to the voice not of the bourbon inspired master of ceremonies but of a much humbled veteran of the march who cautions that we are burning the body and blood of Christ in Vietnam.

What emerges is Mailer's interpretation of the march. In Mailer's view, the demonstrators are visited with grace as they sit face-to-face with the soldiers: ". . . some hint of a glorious future may have hung in the air, some refrain from all the great American rites of passage when men and women manacled themselves to a lost and painful principle and survived a day, a night, a week, a month, a year . . ." These "tender, drug-vitiated jargon-mired children" (280) endure a night which begins in "joy" but includes the terror of military attack. Those who remain to the end are subtly transformed: ". . . they were forever different in the morning than they had been before the night, which is the meaning of a rite of passage, one has voyaged through a channel of shipwreck and temptation . . . some part of the man has been born again, and is better" (280-81). Where Mailer has come through his experience "one suspicion of a whole man closer to that freedom from dread which occupied the inner drama of his years," these flower children and fledgling revolutionaries are forever different in the morning than they had been before the night. The particular experience of book one is generalized in book two. The knot of nihilism is untied, if not "forever" at least for the moment.

This is the "mystery" Mailer discovers in the March on the Pentagon, first in his own experience, then in the collective experience of the demonstrators. Transcending the count of bodies, the tactical success or failure of the demonstration, there is the spiritual renewal attested to by the now impersonal narrative voice of *Armies*.

Perhaps the most important contribution of book one is that it makes this voice possible as the achieved result of the experience recorded there. Therefore Norman Mailer—dwarf alter ego of Lyndon Johnson himself (49)—can plausibly conclude his book with the moving image of "naked Quakers on the cold floor of a dark isolation cell in D.C. jail," and a question almost worthy of Jeremiah, "Did they pray, these Quakers, for forgiveness of the nation? Did they pray with tears in their eyes in those blind cells with visions of a long column of Vietnamese dead, Vietnamese walking a column of flame, eyes on fire, nose on fire, mouth speaking flame . . ." (287). Finally, Mailer can leave us with nothing less than his own prayer for America: "Deliver us from our curse. For we must end on the road to that mystery where courage, death, and the dream of love give promise of sleep" (288). Mailer's narrative has left us on that road, for having presented a vivid and brilliantly annotated account of our condition as a people, Mailer leaves us with the images of young demonstrators undergoing their rite of passage and Quakers praying for the forgiveness of sins: images bearing witness to courage and a dream of love in the face of our death as God's chosen country.

CHAPTER 7

After Armies: *Mailer's Recent Nonfiction*

MAILER'S literary career has had almost as many ups and downs as his well publicized personal life. The early stages of this career are by now almost legendary: early success with *The Naked and the Dead;* decline and fall with *Barbary Shore* and *The Deer Park;* self-announced resurrection with *Advertisements for Myself,* followed by ten years in which Mailer "wasted" his novelistic talents on grubby journalism, only to justify his apparent vagrancy by writing *The Armies of the Night,* one of the more distinguished works of the 1960s. My concern in this chapter is not to reexamine these earlier "periods," but to begin the evaluation of Mailer's most recent phase, what I would half seriously call his post-*Armies* period. This period curiously resembles that ten-year "gap" between Mailer's third novel, *The Deer Park,* and his fourth, *An American Dream,* for Mailer has again gone a full decade without producing a novel while publishing so much journalism that even Mailer specialists have had trouble keeping track of it all. No less than thirteen volumes have appeared since *Armies,* so this would seem to be an even more productive period than Mailer's last respite from novel writing—until one notices that a few of the more recent books (*The Idol and the Octopus, Some Honorable Men*) are in fact Mailer's earlier writings reassembled; that the latest miscellany (*Existential Errands*) is distinctly unworthy of its three predecessors; that the two fight accounts (*King of the Hill, The Fight*) are inferior to "Ten Thousand Words a Minute"; and that the two major examples of Mailer's "engaged" reportage (*Miami and the Siege of Chicago, Of a Fire on the Moon*) are unequal to their model, *The Armies of the Night.* Indeed, anyone who looks closely enough will notice that the recent Mailer has even published a "book" expounding the philosophical assumptions behind graffiti![1] All of which suggests that we may indeed have a new Mailer "period" in the work done between 1968 and 1976, but if so it is a period which calls for discreet silence, not critical evaluation.

129

Benign neglect will not do, however—Mailer is too important a writer and his recent works, both the good and the bad, are far too interesting to be ignored. My own discussion will try to establish three points: that *Miami and the Siege of Chicago* (1968) and *Of a Fire on the Moon* (1970), so successful in their parts, ultimately fail for reasons not yet fully understood; that *The Prisoner of Sex* (1971) and *Marilyn* (1973), though hardly major performances, are much better than has generally been thought; and that Mailer's most distinguished work in this period has been done in the unlikely genre of literary criticism. In general, then, I hope to explain, not simply assert, the limitations of Mailer's recent works, and to establish what in this body of writing deserves a more sympathetic reception than it has yet received.

I   *Miami, Chicago, and the Moon: The Age of Aquarius*

Jimmy Baldwin once entertained the readers of *Esquire* with a sweet and generously written piece called *The Black Boy Looks at the White Boy* in which he talked a great deal about himself and a little bit about me, a proportion I thought well-taken since he is on the best of terms with Baldwin and digs next to nothing about this white boy. As a method, I think it has its merits (*TPP*, 87).

Mailer remarked upon the method of Baldwin's essay in 1962, and everything he has written since confirms that he understands very well the "merits" of Baldwin's approach. Indeed, I have devoted the last two chapters to tracing the evolution of this method from Mailer's earliest essays to *The Armies of the Night*. With the publication of *Armies*, however, Mailer did not abandon his commitment to a "subjective" form of historical writing. To the contrary, Mailer's many recent books all suggest that for him, at least, a work of nonfiction will have conviction only if its author is clearly on whatever stage he happens to be describing. Yet the extent of Mailer's authorial presence differs greatly in his latest works. Only in *Miami and the Siege of Chicago* and *Of a Fire on the Moon* do we find a method truly comparable to that of *The Armies of the Night*. It is natural, then, that we should judge these two books in the light of Mailer's achievement in *Armies*. Such a comparison should underscore both the virtues and the very real limitations of the later works.

The virtues of these books have been widely acknowledged. Essentially, they are the virtues of a supremely interesting journalism. Mailer resisted the generic label "journalist" with some heat in *Armies* and *Of a Fire on the Moon*, but he has come in more recent years to accept it.[2] *Miami and the Siege of Chicago* offers the most vivid and comprehensive published account of the 1968 nominating conventions, while *Of a Fire on the Moon* is a remarkable reconstruction of the Apollo 11 moon shot. Each book is studded with descriptions and characterizations any novelist would envy, let alone any journalist. The history and architecture of Miami Beach, Nelson Rockefeller's arrival in Miami, the stockyards of Chicago, the enigmatic candidacy of Eugene McCarthy, the police attack on demonstrators outside Chicago's Hilton Hotel—these and other phenomena described in *Miami and the Siege of Chicago* allow Mailer to exercise that "phenomenal talent for recording the precise look and feel of things" first praised by Norman Podhoretz twenty-five years ago.[3] Indeed, Mailer's portrait of McCarthy, in "The Siege of Chicago," is the equal of any character study in his novels. Mailer has always been at his reportorial best in dealing with political conventions, as witnessed by his essays on the 1960 Democratic convention, the 1964 Republican convention, and the 1972 nominating conventions (*St. George and the Godfather*), but *Miami and the Siege of Chicago* is his most compelling treatment of the men and movements which constitute contemporary history. And from a journalistic perspective, *Of a Fire on the Moon* is an even more stunning achievement, especially in those sections which describe the Vehicle Assembly Building at Cape Kennedy, the blast-off of Saturn-Apollo, and the craters of the moon.

The virtues of these books are not merely descriptive in nature, however. Even more impressive are those speculative passages inspired by the concrete observation of men and events. At certain points in both works, we hear the unmistakable cadence of Mailer at his prophetic best. Mailer has many other voices, of course—some shrill, some egomaniacal—but this particular voice is heard whenever his shrewdness and lyrical intensity are happily joined. In *Of a Fire on the Moon*, it is heard most clearly in the concluding chapter, "A Burial by the Sea," where Mailer manages to blend reflections on the end of his fourth marriage with thoughts on our exploration of space to form a deeply moving meditation on the state of America at the end of the 1960s. In *Miami and the Siege of Chicago*, it emerges at many points in the narrative, most notably when Mailer watches the Republican leadership file into their grand gala and is moved to reflect on the nature and fate of America's Wasps:

Yet he felt himself unaccountably filled with a mild sorrow. He did not detest these people, he did not feel so superior as to pity them, it was rather he felt a sad sorrowful respect. In their immaculate cleanliness, in the somewhat antiseptic odors of their astringent toilet water and perfume, in the abnegation of their walks, in the heavy sturdy moves so many demonstrated of bodies in life's harness, there was the muted tragedy of the Wasp— they were not on earth to enjoy or even perhaps to love so very much, they were here to serve, and serve they had in public functions and public charities (while recipients of their charity might vomit in rage and laugh in scorn), served on opera committees, and served in long hours of duty at the piano, served as the sentinel in concert halls and the pews on the aisle in church, at the desk in schools, had served for culture, served for finance, served for salvation, served for America—and so much of America did not wish them to serve any longer, and so many of them doubted themselves, doubted that the force of their faith could illumine their path in these new modern horror-head times. On and on, they came through the door, the clean, the well-bred, the extraordinarily prosperous, and for the most astonishing part, the almost entirely proper. . . . now they were subdued, now they were modest, now they were looking for a leader to bring America back to them, their lost America, Jesus-land (MC, 35-36).

I quote at such length to give a fair example of Mailer's meditative technique at its best. Surely it is at moments like these, if ever, that we sympathize with Mailer's celebrated contention that he is "the best writer in America."[4]

But no one has ever based this claim on a reading of Miami and the Siege of Chicago and Of a Fire on the Moon as wholes, so it is necessary to ask why these books seem less successful than The Armies of the Night. It is not, I think, because Armies surpasses the later works in the quality of its reportage or the intensity of its meditative passages. If this is true, it is true only in degree and relatively slight degree at that. Nor is it because Armies provided Mailer with inherently richer material, as so many discussions of the book suggest. In point of fact, the March on the Pentagon was probably less significant, historically, than either the political conventions of 1968 or the mission of Apollo 11. To be fair, those who point to the "richness" of Mailer's material are thinking of the actions undertaken by Mailer as participant rather than the march itself. Robert Solotaroff thus explains Mailer's relative failure in "Nixon in Miami": "The Republican convention offered the reporter no opportunity for dramatic action and so few for dramatic thought that except for a small crisis involving his feelings about Negroes, the most his inner drama could offer hung upon his ruminating about whether

Nixon had really changed."[5] But if we adopt this point of view, what are we to say about "The Siege of Chicago," where Mailer's opportunities for dramatic action are shown to have been legion, yet his published account also fails to match the level of *Armies*? I don't mean to deny the problems Mailer faced in dramatizing the somewhat intractable materials of the Nixon convention or, even more obviously, the Apollo 11 moon shot. But I cannot see that these problems are inherently greater than those Mailer had to deal with in writing about the March on the Pentagon. It is simply that in the case of *Armies* Mailer *solved* his problems.

I have already argued that Mailer did this by employing numerous fictional techniques toward the end of illuminating his subject, the March on the Pentagon. This might not seem an interpretive key, for most of these devices are also used in the later works, but the most crucial of these techniques is precisely what is missing in *Miami and the Siege of Chicago* and *Of a Fire on the Moon:* a conscious shaping of the given materials to form a dramatic action. It is no accident that *Armies* moves from "pugnacious personal comedy to prophetic witness and litany,"[6] for only through some such movement could Mailer present his final conclusions about the march with that prophetic authority he has sought throughout his career. As I have shown in chapter six, Mailer earns this authority by first depicting, in book one, the somewhat comical initiation undergone in the course of the march by his hero, "Norman Mailer," who then returns in the form of a chastened, "objective" narrator for the historical treatment of the demonstration which follows in book two. This rather elaborate procedure is hardly that of the average journalist, who tends to stick doggedly to the chronological order of events, however unclimactic this might be. Nonetheless, it is the key to the extraordinary effect of *Armies*, especially in the concluding chapters; and while it is true that Mailer also deviates from strict chronological development in his later works, he does so there for relatively minor, local effects, not in the service of a pervasive rhetorical strategy. What Jack Richardson says about the author of *Miami and the Siege of Chicago* could also be said of the man who wrote *Of a Fire on the Moon* and *St. George and the Godfather:* "He becomes less and less concerned with maintaining a literary center . . . and allows the sequences from Miami to Chicago to unfold for the most part unchallenged by his imagination."[7]

Richardson's criticism is most relevant to "Nixon in Miami," for this section of *Miami and the Siege of Chicago* is almost literally a *report* on the 1968 Republican convention. Occasionally Mailer alters the chronology of events to permit continuous treatment of Nixon's presence at the convention, or Rockefeller's, but for the most part he has given us a seventy-page description of the convention's daily proceedings. This is in contrast not only to his strategy in *Armies*, but also to his practice in such essays as "In The Red Light," where the events of a political convention become the stages in a personal drama. "In The Red Light" dramatizes Mailer's internal debate with America's warring social forces, particularly those forces represented by the Goldwaterites. It is through such debate that Mailer arrives at a clarified vision of the country, the end he has sought from the first and the factor that determines which events are to be represented. In "Nixon in Miami," we get a radically reduced version of this strategy. Again Mailer introduces himself into his narrative, this time as "the reporter"; again he offers his impressions as an eyewitness; again he dramatizes his attempt to comprehend the convention's "meaning." But as Solotaroff suggests, there isn't much to dramatize. In Miami, Mailer tells us, "the reporter had moved through the convention quietly, as anonymously as possible, wan, depressed, troubled" (*MC*, 14). This modest movement fails to provide the personal drama which unified *Armies* and the earlier convention pieces, so Mailer settles for describing, event after event, what passed before his eyes as he made his anonymous way through the heart of Republican politics. Mailer is indeed curious about the possibility of a "new Nixon," but his engagement with this issue hardly structures his account. At the end Mailer doesn't know "if the candidate were real as a man, or whole as a machine, lonely in his sad eminence or megalomaniacal" (*MC*, 82), and his retrospective treatment of the convention offers few hints which might allow the reader to achieve a more definitive insight.

The problem with "Nixon in Miami" is structural, for the lack of a "literary center" reduces the work to the level of superior journalism. A subtler form of the same problem arises with Mailer's treatment of the 1968 Democratic convention. After an introductory description of Chicago, Mailer devotes the first forty pages of "The Siege of Chicago" to the political forces at work in the convention, an account climaxed by his report on the debate among McCarthy, McGovern, and Humphrey before the California delegation. He then moves outside convention hall to what he calls the real "event" (*MC*, 131) of the convention, the confrontation between Mayor Daley's police and the demonstrators who have come to protest Lyndon Johnson's war policies. Mailer gives fifty pages to describing the demonstrators, their first engagements with the police, and finally the infamous police attack outside the Hilton Hotel on the third day of the convention. Then, fully ninety pages into "The Siege of Chicago," Mailer shifts to his personal role in the convention. From this point to the end of the work, he depicts his own activities, including his several speeches to the demonstrators, his efforts to organize a protest march of unhappy delegates, and his contretemps with the National Guard the last night of the convention. In order to present his three narrative "movements," Mailer must of course move back and forth over the chronological events of the convention, thus emphasizing that he has consciously shaped his narrative. But toward what end?

Since Mailer concludes "The Siege of Chicago" with his own "story," it would seem that he meant to emphasize his personal reactions to the convention. Yet he tells us at one point that "we are concerned with his actions only as they illumine the event of the Republican Convention in Miami, the Democratic Convention in Chicago, and the war of the near streets" (*MC*, 197). This passage describes the persona's role in *Armies*, but curiously fails to square with Mailer's practice in the work he is actually characterizing. If the reporter's actions are to illumine the Democratic convention in Chicago, why are they presented only toward the end, where they receive the emphasis which goes with climactic placement? Do they "illumine" the convention or do they in fact provide a quite different focus? Mailer's procedure here reverses his strategy in *Armies* and reverts to what he did so successfully in the last fifteen pages of "Ten Thousand Words a Minute." In the essay, however, Mailer's personal story is developed throughout the work, not just at the end. The last forty pages of "The Siege of Chicago" read too much like a separate narrative within the work as a whole. Indeed, the real problem here is that "The Siege of Chicago" reads very much like *three* separate narratives, all related by time and place but insufficiently united by an encompassing narrative structure.

This criticism assumes that Mailer's account of his own activities fails to illuminate the convention's meaning. If such illumination was intended, Mailer has been far too reticent about making the necessary connections. I would suggest that Mailer faced an artistic dilemma at this point and indeed throughout the book. Early in "Nixon in Miami" he remarks that the American political scene is dominated by "Left-wing demons, white and Black, working to inflame the conservative heart of America, while Right-wing devils exacerbated Blacks and drove the mind of the New Left and liberal middle class into prides of hopeless position" (*MC*, 15). It is clear that Mailer finds himself squarely in the middle, threatened on both sides by these unattractive political extremes. But of course this is precisely the position he was in a year earlier, at the March on the Pentagon. *The Armies of the Night* dramatizes Mailer's efforts to adjudicate between the ignorant armies of left and right; indeed, it dramatizes the internal debate of a "Left Conservative" who is drawn to both sides in the battle. Was Mailer to describe this struggle again, just one year later? Such repetition would horrify him more than any other literary sin, for he has prided himself on the variety of his works, the fact that he never repeats himself.[8] Yet Mailer's longstanding distaste for "straight" reportage—plus the vicissitudes of his ego—seem to have dictated his presence on the reported scene. Thus we get that relatively anonymous figure, "the reporter." This persona isn't to be regretted altogether for without him we would lack such splendid moments as Mailer's conversations with Eugene McCarthy. But the fact remains that Mailer's perfunctory development of his own activities deprives his work of an organizing principle significantly different from that of "pure" journalism.

Possibly I have misconstrued Mailer's dilemma. What I have said implies that Mailer *could* have focused *Miami and the Siege of Chicago* in the same manner as *The Armies of the Night*, but chose not to do so to avoid repetition. There may have been less choice involved than I suggest. Mailer structured *Armies* around what I have called his "internal debate" because this debate was finally resolved. When he came to see the final moments of the March on the Pentagon as a true *rite de passage* for the demonstrators, Mailer was able to present his participation in the march as leading to a richly climactic insight. He may present no such dramatic movement in *Miami and the Siege of Chicago* because, quite simply, no such resolution occurred. Mailer sides with the demonstrators, as he finally did in *Armies*, but is disinclined to see their confrontation with the police in the same light as the occupation of the Pentagon. Because Mailer's brilliant account of the police attack outside the Hilton Hotel offers no ultimate clarification, it occurs fifty pages before the end of the book. We can only speculate as to why Mailer responded so differently to the events in Washington and Chicago, but I think the answer lies in that growing personal conservatism noted in chapter five. This growth was well advanced by 1967, as witnessed by Mailer's hostility toward the liberals and new leftists who make up one of the "armies" in *The Armies of the Night*. At that time, however, Mailer's radical spirit was sufficiently intact to overcome, in the course of the march, his sometimes querulous, sometimes shrewd objections to the demonstrators. This made possible the resolution already noticed, both in Mailer's personal feelings and in the book he went on to write. One year later, however, the balance has shifted, Mailer's "Left Conservatism" is very conservative indeed, and our author can only record with sorrow and journalistic detachment "the war of the near streets."

Mailer describes this "war" with great skill, but it is the skill of a gifted journalist who is more or less content to let the facts speak for themselves. In Mailer's next book, *Of a Fire on the Moon,* this characteristic is even more pronounced. Indeed, the problems of this work are so similar to those already discussed in relation to *Miami and the Siege of Chicago,* I will restrict my remarks to Mailer's failure to transcend the narrative structure of a report—in this case, almost five hundred pages long!

Of a Fire on the Moon is formally divided into three parts. Part I, "Aquarius," presents Mailer's eyewitness account of the final preparations for Apollo 11 and the awesome blast-off; part II, "Apollo," describes the mission in voluminous and technical detail, from its inception to the recovery of its astronauts; part III, "The Age of Aquarius," returns to Mailer's coverage of the mission via television, at the same time that his fourth marriage is deteriorating, and concludes with his thoughts on the significance of it all. This structure would seem to resemble that of Mailer's better essays in which he begins and ends with his own relation to an event described in the middle of the work. This resemblance is finally seen to be superficial, however. In an essay like "Ten Thousand Words a Minute," for example, the concluding section resolves both personal and more general issues raised by Mailer's participation in the reported event. Thus we experience our "sense of an ending," as Frank Kermode would have it, on both the essay's dramatic and intellectual levels. In *Of a Fire on the Moon,* part III returns us to an essentially unchanged observer who is perplexed by the same unanswered questions he had brought to the mission in part I. Mailer has again structured his work around his role as reporter; but the dramatic implications are never realized, for there is literally no dramatic movement.

Mailer refers to himself here as Aquarius, a persona he will characterize in *St. George and the Godfather* as "modest and half-invisible" (p. 3). Aquarius is a man who has "learned to live with questions"; he is sufficiently detached from "the imperial demands of his ego" to become "an acolyte to technology" (*Fire,* 4, 6, 56) and describe an event advertised as the "triumph" of twentieth-century science. Indeed, he is so adept at living with questions and so detached from the demands of his ego that for the most part he is *entirely* invisible. Certainly nothing happens to him which Mailer can use to focus his account of the moon shot. We might therefore expect *Of a Fire on the Moon* to be as modest in its proportions as its "hero." Instead, Mailer has filled the middle section of his typical structure with nothing less than three hundred pages on the mechanics of Apollo 11, perhaps the longest description of a single event in literary history. It is as if Mailer would somehow conceal the fact that he has nothing to dramatize by expanding to heroic proportions what is usually a subordinate section in his essays. A similar strategy seems at work in Mailer's endless reiteration of *the* question posed by Apollo 11: does our effort in space serve God or the devil? Richard Poirier has suggested that Mailer's recent works use the unresolved dualisms in such questions as a kind of literary crutch.[9] It is fitting that *Of a Fire on the Moon* is his first example, for Mailer's many variations on this question seem calculated to substitute for the dramatic insights experienced by other, less invisible personae in his earlier works.

Mailer's dilemma here recalls his problem in *Miami and the Siege of Chicago.* His personal experience of the event in question either led to a climactic insight or it did not—Mailer was in either case in a losing position. Without a climactic insight he would have to make do with the tactics of superior journalism. With it, he had to confront the unappealing prospect of repeating the successful narrative strategy of *Armies.* "Once a philosopher, twice a pervert," as Mailer has so often remarked, quoting Voltaire. *Miami and the Siege of Chicago* and *Of a Fire on the Moon* therefore suggest the limitations of Mailer's subjective approach to nonfiction so far as the reporting of historical events is concerned. These limitations suggest in turn that for Mailer to continue with this approach in the 1970s he would have to find other materials upon which to apply it. I think that *The Prisoner of Sex* and *Marilyn* are the literary results of just such a search.[10]

II *Prisoners of Sex: Mailer and Monroe*

The Prisoner of Sex and *Marilyn* have many things in common. Each is centrally concerned with women, a subject Mailer had never before placed at the heart of his work. Each was received with great critical chagrin. Indeed, each was a kind of *cause célèbre;* for the initial publication of *The Prisoner of Sex* in *Harper's* (May, 1971) led to the dismissal of the magazine's editor, Willie Morris, while the appearance of *Marilyn* provoked many accusations that Mailer had defiled the memories of Marilyn Monroe and the Kennedys, Jack and Bobby. The two works are related in other, more literary ways, however. Most crucially, each book represents Mailer's attempt to find a different use for those nonfictional techniques he developed during the 1960s. In *The Prisoner of Sex*, Mailer employs these techniques in the service of an extended philosophical essay; in *Marilyn*, he uses them to enrich a formal biography. Neither effort is altogether successful, but each represents a modest success we could never anticipate from the massive literary gossip which accompanied its publication.

Mailer's success in *The Prisoner of Sex* is so modest that it has escaped the notice of even sympathetic readers. Among unsympathetic readers, the only issue has been whether Mailer's persona or his thought is the more objectionable. Brigid Brophy's description of the book as "an appreciative meditation by Norman Mailer on Norman Mailer"[11] calls attention to the fact that Mailer has once again introduced a self-portrait into his nonfiction. Because *The Prisoner of Sex* does not report an historical event and in fact has all the trappings of a philosophical essay, we might first ask why "Mailer" is in the work at all.

The role of Mailer's persona can be seen as quite familiar. In this view, Mailer again thrusts himself forward as a representative figure, though here he represents only the male half of the population. Mailer refers to himself as the PW, which stands for Prisoner of Wedlock (a four-time loser!) or Prizewinner. He explains that these are "polar concepts to be regarded at opposite ends of his ego" (*PS*, 9), but they can also be seen as his credentials for undertaking a philosophical examination of women in general and Women's Liberation in particular. As one who has known the intimate trials of marriage and the masculine world of work, Mailer is prepared to represent the male point of view on our most recent version of the war between the sexes. He offers his qualifications in section one, proceeds to examine literary manifestations of feminine unrest in section two, conducts an extended attack on his feminine counterpart, Kate Millett, in section three, and concludes with a meditation on masculinity and femininity in section four. This structure suggests that hostile readers are right to see the book as an elaborate self-defense; but it should also be said that Mailer's self-portrait focuses what might otherwise have been a hopelessly abstract philosophical inquiry. (Given Mailer's views, it is sufficiently abstract, even mystical, in its published form.)

Mailer achieves this focus at great cost, however. It is one thing to be an eccentric but representative American, Mailer's role in such works as "Ten Thousand Words a Minute," "In The Red Light," and *The Armies of the Night*. It is quite another to be a representative male chauvinist. This role is too confining, too partisan, to illuminate the issue in question. Very simply, Mailer's role is such that we finish *The Prisoner of Sex* knowing a good deal more about his idiosyncratic view of the world than about Women's Liberation. This problem is compounded by Mailer's decision to treat Kate Millett as a representative feminist. Nothing in *The Prisoner of Sex* is more effective than Mailer's attack on Millett's treatment of Henry Miller, D. H. Lawrence, and Jean Genet (not to mention Norman Mailer) in her book *Sexual Politics*,[12] but the most sympathetic reader must finally wonder whether Kate Millett is an adequate opponent. Read out of context, the third section of *The Prisoner of Sex* is a superb example of Mailer's gift for literary criticism; read in context, it has the look of a personal quarrel gratuitously elevated to the level of an exemplary debate between male and female. Indeed, Mailer's "victory" over Millett is even counterproductive, as one of Mailer's despised technocrats might say, for it gives rise to the suspicion that Mailer has avoided the more difficult task of confronting a truly formidable feminist.

These criticisms are valid, I think, insofar as *The Prisoner of Sex* aspires to be an objective critique of feminism, specifically Women's Liberation. In point of fact, however, Mailer's pretensions in this direction are only intermittently pursued. Ultimately, Mailer's persona represents nothing more inclusive than his own instinctive biases. The result is a much more personal, less ambitious work than we expect from Mailer. The positive side to this is that judged by these more modest standards *The Prisoner of Sex* is relatively successful: well written, often humorous, agreeably structured around its author's response to the women's movement. The negative side is that Mailer's personal views cannot be argued away as a means of ironic self-characterization. Here these views are the immediate occasion for Mailer's essay, the full burden of what he would like to communicate. For many readers, this is a heavy burden indeed.

Mailer's views on women, as expressed here and throughout his works, have been attacked by any number of critics, perhaps most successfully by Jean Radford.[13] I don't wish to defend Mailer's views, but think it fair to add that they are more complex than is usually acknowledged. Mailer does believe that men and women are inherently different, that "man is alienated from the nature which brought him forth, he is not like woman in possession of an inner space which gives her link to the future" (*PS*, 111). For Mailer, man defines himself by what he *does*, woman by what she *is*. Thus he can say that "nobody was born a man; you earned manhood provided you were good enough, bold enough" (*Armies*, p. 25). Mailer resents the feminist's "dull assumption that the sexual force of a man was the luck of his birth, rather than his finest moral product" (*PS*, 45). Of course, he is quite willing to assume that a woman's sexual force—derived from her "inner space"—is precisely the luck of her birth, rather than her finest moral product. The contradiction is glaring, but it should be seen as rooted in Mailer's insistence on the biological foundation to all human realities, even those we tend to think of as conventional or moral. As Radford points out, this all too closely resembles the view that men and women are inherently different because God made them that way.[14]

Mailer's distrust of Women's Liberation is not simply based on chauvinistic cliches, however. He also fears that feminist ideas are "artfully designed to advance the fortunes of the oncoming technology of the state" (*PS*, 50). Mailer has in mind feminist advocacy of test-tube babies, or indeed any attempt to alleviate the burdens of childbearing and childcare by technological means. He can be accused of acute paranoia in his attitude toward modern science—he would even have us suffer headaches rather than use aspirin!—but this is hardly a simple form of male chauvinism.

To continue this dissection of Mailer's views on women would be cruel and unusual punishment, however; for the best that can be said about *The Prisoner of Sex* is that it is much better than its critics have insisted. It is *Marilyn* that deserves serious reconsideration. The excellence of Mailer's biography of Marilyn Monroe has been all but overlooked in the hoopla that attended its publication and the subsequent charge of plagiarism by Maurice Zolotow, one of Mailer's sources.[15] *Marilyn* is perhaps the most curious of Mailer's relative successes, for it is his one book which succeeds by rejecting those grandiose ambitions characterizing his other works. That it does avoid crippling excesses, that it is almost surely the best written of Mailer's works since *Armies*—these points need to be affirmed in the wake of the book's short lived notoriety.

It may seem perverse to argue that one of *Marilyn's* virtues is its modesty, for Mailer begins the book by asserting Monroe's exemplary status. Her suicide is cited as one of those "deaths and spiritual disasters" (M, 16) which epitomize the 1960s; she is said to represent an entire generation: "In her ambition, so Faustian, and in her ignorance of culture's dimensions, in her liberation and her tyrannical desires, her noble democratic longings intimately contradicted by the widening pool of her narcissism (where every friend and slave must bathe), we can see the magnified mirror of ourselves, our exaggerated and now all but defeated generation" (M, 17). Indeed, Mailer even refers to Monroe as "the last of the myths to thrive in the long evening of the American dream" (M, 16). Such a prologue must create apocalyptic expectations in readers who know nothing of Mailer's other works; readers familiar with those works must anticipate a book in the same vein as "Ten Thousand Words a Minute," in which Floyd Patterson and Sonny Liston are seen as representatives of the Lord and Satan, respectively, or "Superman Comes to the Supermarket," in which Jack Kennedy is cast as the American hero incarnate. Surprisingly, however, Mailer's book sticks very much to its first announced goal—to pursue "the identity of a lovely if seldom simple woman" (M, 9). Whether Mailer captures that identity is arguable, but at least he never abandons the flesh-and-blood Monroe in pursuit of some grander, more inclusive hypothesis about contemporary America. Mailer's concern for the "real" Monroe is such that even the reviewer for Ms. magazine praised "the passionate effort of mind and feeling which he applies . . . to really knowing what it must feel like to be a woman."[16]

I don't mean to suggest that Mailer has restricted his role to the purveying of facts. Mailer once remarked that "he could not engage in a creative act without a set of major theses to support him" (EE, 98), and Marilyn is a book filled with major and minor theses: about Monroe, of course, but also about film, acting, Hollywood, Joe DiMaggio, Arthur Miller, and the other men in Monroe's life. At one point Mailer even pushes forward a notion he first advanced in a discussion of his own ventures into filmmaking: "Film is a phenomenon whose resemblance to death has been ignored too long" (EE, 134; M, 177). But this unhappy preface to a dissertation on film is soon abandoned in the pursuit of Monroe's difficult identity. Indeed, the most infamous of Mailer's theses—that Monroe may have been killed by a rightwing element in the government which sought to embarrass Bobby Kennedy—is a tentatively presented, all but insignificant detail in the work as a whole. For the most part, Mailer's theses are limited to crucial matters in Monroe's life. Because they derive from the facts of that life, they are immediately relevant to Mailer's goal of writing "a novel biography" (*M*, 15).

Mailer's intentions as a "novel biographer" are not so pretentious as the phrase might suggest. Certainly he does not want to create fictions where facts once reigned; one of his continuing concerns is to distinguish the facts of Monroe's life from what he calls "factoids" ("facts which have no existence before appearing in a magazine or newspaper"—*M*, 18). As a novel biographer, he seeks to comprehend the reliable facts concerning Monroe in order to present "a literary hypothesis of a *possible* Marilyn Monroe who might actually have lived and fit most of the facts available" (*M*, 20). He wants to write a version of "psycho-history" (*M*, 19) in which Monroe's complex character is explained to his own satisfaction and that of his more sympathetic readers. This involves Mailer in a good many specula-tions, of course, as when he tells us that "there is no way to comprehend Monroe unless we assume that her deepest experience in life was the act of playing in a superb role" (*M*, 130). But this particular surmise grows out of Monroe's well documented concern for her acting career and illustrates the kind of speculative freedom we grant other, less controversial biographers as a matter of course.

Mailer begins by remarking that Monroe has always been pre-sented as either "an angelic and sensitive victim or a murderous emotional cripple" (*M*, 23). It seems clear to him that she was both; his book is an attempt to discover that "literary hypothesis" which will do justice to her all but schizophrenic character. Mailer departs from previous biographers by searching for his hypothesis in Monroe's films as well as her personal life. The major conclusion he draws from the films is that Monroe was a great actress, a great *artist*, whose theatrical ambitions were as crucial to her tragedy as her dismal childhood. This is so for two reasons: the men in her life were insensitive to her talent, and she cultivated her great ambition with almost no sense of an "inner identity" (*M*, 126). Lacking such a sense, inevitably exploited by those who could not understand her, Monroe was doomed to a series of self-destructive acts which anticipated her suicide. Most of *Marilyn* is devoted to justifying these claims. Mailer works carefully through the available information on Monroe's affairs and marriages and the various pieces of evidence which support his crucial contention that Monroe, for all her egotism, lacked a solid sense of identity. Ultimately, Mailer's success or failure depends on whether he has satisfied the most common demand we make on biographers: that their evidence support their accompanying conjectures.

It is a matter of opinion, of course, as to whether or not Mailer has succeeded. I have argued that he tries to succeed by means entirely consistent with the biographer's task. I would add that if Mailer has not "captured" Monroe, he has come closer than anyone else. This view derives in part from Mailer's impressive discussion of Monroe's films, especially his lengthy treatment of *The Misfits*; for these discussions suggest that Mailer's hypothesis is superior precisely because it incorporates the artistic side of her character. It also derives from Mailer's painstaking consideration of Monroe's men, who are so persuasively etched they seem like the most realistic characters in a realistic novel. Again and again Mailer brings Monroe's relationships to life, as when he remarks of Joe DiMaggio, "He will found a dynasty with her if she desires it, but he does not see their love as a tender wading pool of shared interests and tasting each other's concoctions in the kitchen" (*M*, 100). Yes, we come to feel, this is a marriage which prepares a certain kind of personality for suicide. There are a hundred such passages in *Marilyn*, each based on information to be found in other biographies but transformed by Mailer's intensely sympathetic yet considered reflection.

Like *The Prisoner of Sex*, then, *Marilyn* succeeds by pursuing certain limited ends with a kind of professional purity. If *Marilyn* is the more impressive achievement, it is perhaps because Mailer is right when he argues that only another artist can comprehend Monroe: "Set a thief to catch a thief, and put an artist on an artist" (*M*, 20). This is a proposition we will encounter again, in the even more impressive context of Mailer's literary criticism.

III   *Mailer as Literary Critic*

There is something incongruous—even depressing—about the fact that Mailer's most successful work in the last ten years has been literary criticism. I may be exaggerating the incongruity, since Mailer has been publishing literary criticism for twenty years now; but to argue that Mailer's best work in the 1970s is to be found in a few literary essays is to acknowledge the relatively minor dimensions of this period. Still, we must follow wherever Mailer's career leads us, and it remains a stubborn fact that Mailer's recent criticism poses none of the aesthetic problems which mark even such interesting books as *Miami and the Siege of Chicago* and *Of a Fire on the Moon*.

For the most part, its limitations are those of the form Mailer is employing. Perhaps it is significant that the same can be said of *Marilyn,* for these are the recent works furthest removed from the "engaged" reportage Mailer perfected in the 1960s. Forced to retreat from the successful strategies of his earlier works, Mailer has achieved a limited success in such traditional forms as biography and the literary essay.

From the first Mailer's literary criticism has revealed a decided interest in the writer as opposed to the writer's works. Mailer has cherished no desire to be included among the newer "New Critics": "There is a kind of critic who writes only about the dead. He sees the great writers of the past as simple men. They are born with a great talent, they exercise it, and they die. Such critics see the mastery in the work; they neglect the subtle failures of the most courageous intent, and the dramatic hours when the man took the leap to become a great writer" (*CC,* 108). As these remarks suggest, Mailer usually assesses a writer's *character* rather than "the mastery in the work." He believes that "the writer, particularly the American writer, is not usually—if he is interesting—the quiet master of his craft; he is rather a being who ventured into the jungle of his unconscious to bring back a sense of order or a sense of chaos" (*CC,* 108). Mailer is fascinated by the writer's excursion into this "jungle"—after all, he has made such a journey himself—and finds literary criticism a meaningful activity only when he is dealing with the artist and/or the creative process. The result of this attitude in Mailer's early survey of his contemporaries, "Evaluations—Quick and Expensive Comments on the Talent in the Room" (*Adv,* 463-73), is little more than character assassination. Here James Jones is attacked for his "blind vanity" (*Adv,* 463), J. D. Salinger is rejected as "no more than the greatest mind ever to stay in prep school" (*Adv,* 467), and Chandler Brossard is summed up as "a mean pricky guy who's been around" (*Adv,* 469). But Mailer's method can lead to much better results. Among the earlier essays, I would cite "The Dynamic of American Letters" and "Some Children of the Goddess" (both reprinted in *Cannibals and Christians*). More recently, Mailer has given us excellent analyses of the New York intelligensia and Norman Podhoretz' *Making It* (*EE,* 171-97), the psychological struggles of D. H. Lawrence (*PS,* 134-60), and the "gargantuan talents and vices" (*GL,* x) of Henry Miller. Indeed, Mailer has written several times on Miller in the last few years, and it is this body of work (brought together in *Genius and Lust*) which illustrates his critical intelligence at its best.[17]

Reviewers of *Genius and Lust* have suggested that the book represents a subtle form of self-aggrandizement. Because Mailer's Henry Miller resembles no one so much as Norman Mailer, this argument goes, Mailer's inflated claims for Miller are claims for his own work. This rather unkind theory is based on a genuine biographical connection between critic and subject. Both Mailer and Miller grew up in Brooklyn and devoted their early years to escaping from the vise of middle-class culture; both achieved fame as literary "outlaws" best known for their use of obscene materials; both have experienced the pain of four marriages ending in divorce. (Indeed, each first married a woman named Beatrice!) It is certainly clear that Mailer identifies with Miller. How else are we to account for his remarkable claim that Miller's achievement equals or surpasses that of Melville, Faulkner, Hemingway, and Fitzgerald ("one has to take the English language back to Marlowe and Shakespeare before encountering a wealth of imagery equal in intensity"—*GL*, 4)? But to remark that Mailer sees himself in Henry Miller fails to tell us much about his critical analysis of Miller and his works. Here we have another example of an artist set to catch another artist. Questions of identification aside, does Mailer "catch" anything about Henry Miller that is worth keeping?

Mailer presents a powerful case for Miller as a first-rate talent (though his "ranking" of Miller is no doubt an indulgence). The case is persuasive because Mailer does not shrink away from Miller's faults. In fact, Mailer believes that "it is impossible to talk of a great artist without speaking of failure" (*GL*, xii), the great artist's failure to achieve his inevitably grandiose intentions. Mailer speaks often and eloquently of Henry Miller's failures: the fact that "at his worst, he sounds like a small-town newspaper editorial" (*GL*, 6); the revealing truth that "he could be poetic about anything and everything except fucking with love" (*GL*, xiii); the absence of fully created women in his books, especially in his sixteen-hundred page magnum opus, *The Rosy Crucifixion*. Mailer understands the justice in Miller's description of himself as a man "filled with wisdom and nonsense" (*GL*, xi). He captures the nonsense in Miller as no one ever has, perhaps because he is able to place it in the context of Miller's wisdom.

This wisdom has little to do with Miller's tendency to philosophize, which Mailer rightly deplores as diverting our attention from his real gifts. In Mailer's view, these gifts are essentially those of a superior realist. Miller's genius was for describing areas of human experience, predominantly sexual, untouched by previous writers; his literary salvation was to understand "that no account of an unpleasant event could survive its evasions" (*GL*, 96), that the writer who would engage life's underside must do so wholeheartedly, with something like Miller's gusto, or the attempt will flounder. Mailer is very good at evoking this aspect of Miller—the massive selections from Miller's works are intended to represent it—but he is even more impressive in tracing its sources in Miller's life. The best passages in *Genius and Lust* are true to Mailer's biographical orientation as a critic, describing as they do Miller's struggles with his Germanic background (personified in his mother), his Brooklyn inspired contempt for tender sex and women, his only partially successful efforts to overcome this training, his amazing decision at the age of forty to devote his life to writing unpublishable books, and the gradual emergence of his unique literary posture despite the handicaps of overwhelming poverty and a mere high-school education. Mailer's prolonged treatment of Miller's life illumines the artist as well as the man, for we are finally made to understand both the size of Miller's achievement and its inevitable limitations. This side of Richard Ellmann, few critics have achieved happier results with the biographical method.

It must be admitted that the later sections of *Genius and Lust* are unequal to the earlier ones. Mailer's long essay on Miller is divided into nine introductions to the selections from Miller's books; as the later selections grow shorter and less interesting (thus mirroring the course of Miller's career), Mailer's discussions become hardly more than assembled notes on the later Miller. Even in discussing Miller's less valuable works, however, Mailer illuminates the nature of Miller's *ouevre*. Mailer sees most of the later books as the limited but honorable efforts of a man who will not repeat his early successes:

If he had remained the protagonist by which he first presented himself in *Tropic of Cancer*—the man with iron in his phallus, acid in his mind, and some kind of incomparable relentless freedom in his heart, that paradox of tough misery and keen happiness, that connoisseur of the spectrum of odors between good sewers and bad sewers, that noble rat gnawing on existence and impossible to kill, then he could indeed have been a legend, a species of Parisian Bogart or American Belmondo. Everybody would have wanted to meet this poet-gangster, barbarian-genius (*GL*, 12).

But this is precisely what Miller could not do and remain true to his complex personality. So he went on to write very different works in his later years: literary criticism, reportage, sentimental travel books, hymns to America, jeremiads against America. Mailer argues that the variety of these works must be traced back to the nature of their author, and even those of us skeptical about the critical method involved must find the argument compelling.

We must also recognize the striking parallel between Miller's later works (as Mailer describes them) and Mailer's productions since 1968. The parallel is not necessarily a happy one, for Mailer's pursuit of new forms has also met with either failure or only partial success. Nonetheless, it is important that we honor Mailer's willingness to experiment, to wear many hats (some too large, some too small), for this has made possible his successes as well as his failures. Besides, the books discussed above are only relative "failures"; if they do not satisfy us entirely, it is largely because Mailer has established such a high standard in his earlier works. In their distinctive ways, these books contribute to that ever growing body of work which has made Mailer the most important writer of nonfiction in the postwar period.

CHAPTER 8

Mailer's Career: A Brief Review

W HAT uneasy impetuousness to take a writer in the midst of his career, at the height of his productivity and renown, and attempt to assess what in his work will have permanent value after the literary controversies about the living man have receded from criticism into biography or cultural history," writes Leo Braudy.[1] Anyone who assesses Mailer's "permanent value" must share the reservations expressed in this quotation. Yet Braudy's remarks occur at the beginning of his own attempt to estimate Mailer's place in literary history and thus reflect his uneasiness with a task he knows he must nonetheless undertake. After all, the critic's task is to make just such evaluations. The critic of a still-living, still-productive writer knows that his judgments must be tentative; but he can hardly avoid making them if he is to remain a critic. Thus the critical judgments I have made throughout this book; thus the judgments I am about to make in this brief concluding chapter.

Before offering final words on Mailer, however, I think it only fair to acknowledge once again the assumptions underlying these judgments. This study opened with a few remarks in the preface concerning Richard Poirier's argument that Mailer should not be evaluated in traditional literary terms which emphasize structure and form. One of Mailer's more recent critics, Laura Adams, was so taken with this argument as to have written, "What the work of Poirier and others has established by now is that traditional approaches to Mailer are inadequate. An existential criticism is needed for purposes of evaluation even more than of interpretation of Mailer's work, and such a critical approach would have to accept Mailer's givens as its own and judge him by his own standards rather than insist that he conform to accepted literary tastes and practices."[2]

What is meant here by an "existential criticism" is none too clear, not even to one who has read Adams' book on Mailer. What *is* clear is

149

her desire to protect Mailer from judgments based on "accepted literary tastes and practices" or "traditional" critical approaches. She assumes that Mailer must inevitably be found wanting if judged by such approaches. I can only say that if this is true, so much the worse for Mailer. Accepted literary tastes and practices have usually been accepted for good reasons—reasons which apply to Mailer as much as to any other imaginative writer. Frankly, I think it perverse to argue that traditional critical approaches are "irrelevant" to Mailer, as if his works were so *sui generis* as to be quite outside the boundaries of normal critical analysis. At any rate, I have assumed that Mailer's works must be judged in just those "traditional" literary terms we bring to the study of any writer.

The irony is that, judged in these terms, Mailer comes off very well indeed. Mailer has published over twenty original volumes, so it is hardly surprising that he has written a number of books which are unsuccessful by any standard, "existential" or otherwise. Yet if we cut away what is palpably "minor" in Mailer's collected works, there remains a body of writing for which relatively large claims can be made. Mailer has written two important novels, one of the best works of nonfiction in American literary history, and a body of essays which will stand comparison with the best nonfiction in this century. Even minor works, such as *Marilyn*, and seriously flawed works, such as *Why Are We in Vietnam?*, contribute to Mailer's imposing output of serious and original work. Mailer's contributions in the novel form have not been particularly innovative, but this shouldn't blind us to the virtues of such "traditional" fictions as *The Naked and the Dead* and *The Deer Park*. His claims to originality are stronger in his works of nonfiction, but it is more to the point that he has *succeeded* in so many of these works. Mailer is a writer who can't be judged by a single book, not even *The Armies of the Night*. His appeal today— and, I would venture, his appeal in the future—lies in that sizable body of successful work, fiction and nonfiction alike, analyzed in earlier chapters. He seems to me to stand with Robert Lowell, Saul Bellow, and Thomas Pynchon as one of the four most important American writers of our time. When the literary controversies about the living man have receded, I expect that Mailer and not his many critics will have had the last word.

Notes and References

Preface

1. For these three figures see, respectively, Stanley Edgar Hyman, "Norman Mailer's Yummy Rump," *New Leader*, March 15, 1965, p. 17; Norman Mailer, *Existential Errands* (Boston: Little, Brown and Company, 1972), p. 260; Laura Adams, "Existential Aesthetics: An Interview with Norman Mailer," *Partisan Review*, 42 (1975), 210.

2. Norman Mailer, *Advertisements for Myself* (New York: G. P. Putnam's Sons, 1959), pp. 465–66.

3. "What Might Have Been," *Newsweek*, November 9, 1959, p. 127.

4. Robert C. Healey, "Novelists of the War: A Bunch of Dispossessed," in *Fifty Years of the American Novel: A Christian Appraisal*, ed. Harold C. Gardiner, S. J. (New York: Charles Scribner's Sons, 1951), p. 263; Charles J. Rolo, review of *Advertisements for Myself, Atlantic Monthly*, 204 (December 1959), 168; "What Might Have Been," p. 127.

5. See Edmund Fuller, *Man in Modern Fiction* (New York: Vintage Books, 1958), pp. 101–104, 154–62; Frederick J. Hoffman, "Norman Mailer and the Revolt of the Ego: Some Observations on Recent American Literature," *Wisconsin Studies in Contemporary Literature*, 1 (Autumn 1961), 5–12; George A. Schrader, "Norman Mailer and the Despair of Defiance," *Yale Review*, 51 (December 1961), 267–80; Diana Trilling, "The Radical Moralism of Norman Mailer," *Claremont Essays* (New York: Harcourt Brace Jovanovich, 1962), pp. 175–202.

6. This focus on Mailer's thought can lead to useful insights, of course. Robert Solotaroff's *Down Mailer's Way* (Urbana: University of Illinois Press, 1974) is perhaps the best study of any contemporary American writer, for example. But there is an unmistakable tendency in this kind of criticism to treat Mailer as a quasiphilosopher, rather than as an imaginative writer. For other, less successful examples of this approach to Mailer, see the Adams, Gutman, Kaufmann, and Radford items in my selected bibliography.

7. Harvey Swados, "Must Writers Be Characters?" *Saturday Review*, October 1, 1960, p. 14.

8. See Eve Auchincloss and Nancy Lynch, "An Interview with Norman Mailer," *Mademoiselle*, 52 (February 1961), 76–77, 160–63.

9. See "Americana: Of Time & the Rebel," *Time*, December 5, 1960, pp. 16–17; Dwight Macdonald, "Our Far-Flung Correspondent: Massachusetts vs. Mailer," *New Yorker*, October 8, 1960, pp. 154–66; "The Boston Trial of *Naked Lunch*," *Evergreen Review*, 9 (June 1965), 40–49, 87–88.

10. See Brock Brower, "In This Corner, Norman Mailer, Never the Champion, Always the Challenger," *Life*, September 24, 1965, pp. 94–117; Joseph Roddy, "The Latest Model Mailer," *Look*, May 27, 1969, pp. 22–28; James Toback, "At Play in the Fields of the Bored," *Esquire*, 70 (December 1968), 150–55.

11. *Norman Mailer* (Minneapolis: University of Minnesota Press, 1968), p. 42.

12. *Ibid.*, pp. 42–43.

13. *The Performing Self* (New York: Oxford University Press, 1971), pp. xv, 87. Poirier extends this argument in his book *Norman Mailer* (New York: Viking Press, 1972).

Chapter One

1. See Norman Mailer, *The Armies of the Night* (New York: New American Library, 1968), pp. 5–6.

2. *Ibid.*, p. 77.

3. *Current Biography* (New York: H. W. Wilson Company, 1948), p. 408.

4. "Rugged Times," *New Yorker*, October 23, 1948, p. 25.

5. See *Brushfire*, eds. William Baines and Henry Nuwer (Reno: Associated Students of the University of Nevada, 1973), p. 19.

6. For an excellent book-length treatment of Mailer's shifting intellectual commitments, see Solotaroff's *Down Mailer's Way*.

7. *Deaths for the Ladies (and other disasters)* (New York: G. P. Putnam's Sons, 1962).

8. Mailer has recently discussed his talk-show days in "Of a Small and Modest Malignancy, Wicked and Bristling with Dots," *Esquire*, 88 (November 1977), 125–48.

9. For more on Mailer's mayoralty campaign, see Joe Flaherty, *Managing Mailer* (New York: Coward-McCann, 1969), and Peter Manso, ed., *Running Against the Machine* (Garden City: Doubleday and Company, 1969).

10. The best account of Mailer's quarrel with Women's Liberation is his own *The Prisoner of Sex* (Boston: Little, Brown and Company, 1971). For Mailer's endorsement of a Fifth Estate, see Patricia Bosworth, "Fifth Estate at the Four Seasons," *Saturday Review of the Arts*, March 1973, pp. 5–7.

11. See Adams, "Existential Aesthetics: An Interview with Norman Mailer," p. 212.

12. *Existential Errands*, p. ix.

13. For details concerning the new novel, see Adams, "Existential Aesthetics: An Interview with Norman Mailer," pp. 210–11, 214, and Laura Adams, *Existential Battles: The Growth of Norman Mailer* (Athens: Ohio University Press, 1976), p. 179.

Chapter Two

1. This short novel, "A Calculus at Heaven," is reprinted in *Advertisements for Myself*, pp. 29–70.

2. See *Writers at Work:* The Paris Review *Interviews*, Third Series, ed. George Plimpton (New York: Viking Press, 1967), p. 260.

3. The novel's popular success was such that it remained number one on the *New York Times* best-seller list for eleven weeks (June 22–August 29).

4. "Mailer and Styron: Guests of the Establishment," *Hudson Review*, 17 (August 1964), 347.

5. "War Novelist," *Nation*, June 26, 1948, p. 723.

6. Norman Podhoretz, "Norman Mailer: The Embattled Vision," *Partisan Review*, 26 (Summer 1959), 371.

7. *Current Biography*, p. 410.

8. Harvey Breit, "Talk with Norman Mailer," *New York Times Book Review*, June 3, 1951, p. 20.

9. *Ibid.*

10. See, for example, Ihab Hassan, *Radical Innocence* (New York: Harper & Row, 1961), p. 141; Chester Eisinger, *Fiction of the Forties* (Chicago: University of Chicago Press, 1963), p. 37; Solotaroff, pp. 14, 18. The phrase "young liberal" is Hassan's.

11. See especially Podhoretz, pp. 371–77; Solotaroff, pp. 3–39; Howard M. Harper, Jr., *Desperate Faith* (Chapel Hill: University of North Carolina Press, 1967), pp. 96–103.

12. *The Structured Vision of Norman Mailer* (New York: New York University Press, 1969), pp. 16–17.

13. *The Naked and the Dead* (New York: Holt, Rinehart and Winston, 1948). Unless otherwise noted, page references in this chapter are to this edition.

14. John M. Muste reaches the same conclusion in his "Norman Mailer and John Dos Passos: The Question of Influence," *Modern Fiction Studies*, 17 (Autumn 1971), 361–62.

15. John W. Aldridge, *After the Lost Generation* (New York: McGraw-Hill, 1951), p. 135; *Cannibals and Christians*, p. 112.

16. "The Naked, the Dead, and the Machine: A New Look at Norman Mailer's First Novel," *PMLA*, 87 (March 1972), 273, 276.

17. See Podhoretz, pp. 373–77; Aldridge, *After the Lost Generation*, pp. 136–40.

18. See *Writers at Work:* The Paris Review *Interviews*, Third Series, p. 260.

19. *Ibid.*, p. 257.

20. *Fiction of the Forties*, p. 35.

21. Cummings' self-pity is revealed throughout the novel. See especially pp. 78, 106, 182. For hints more or less overt of his homosexuality, see pp. 80, 83, 173, 322, 388, 408, 425–26.

22. Taken from Nietzsche's *Thus Spake Zarathustra,* "Plant and Phantom" is the title of part three of *The Naked and the Dead.*

23. Eisinger, p. 37.

24. "Rugged Times," p. 25.

25. *Current Biography,* p. 410.

26. See Friedrich Nietzsche, *Thus Spake Zarathustra,* in *The Philosophy of Nietzsche,* ed. Willard Huntington Wright (New York, 1954), p. 6.

27. Mailer also dramatizes this division in his minor characters, especially Roth, Gallagher, Wilson, and Goldstein. My emphasis upon the major characters somewhat distorts the value of these minor figures.

28. Croft's homosexuality is a difficult thing to "prove," but seems to be hinted at all through the book. See especially p. 145.

29. "Norman Mailer: The Embattled Vision," p. 387.

30. Mailer has confessed to a secret admiration for Croft in *The Presidential Papers,* p. 136.

31. For evidence that Cummings does intend to execute Hearn when he assigns him to the I and R platoon, see pp. 401, 717.

32. Aldridge, *After the Lost Generation,* p. 138.

33. Just before his death, Hearn acknowledges the tawdriness of his motives and decides *not* to be like Cummings and Croft (p. 584). He decides to turn in his commission but is murdered before he can make this last and more compelling gesture of rebellion.

34. "Rugged Times," p. 25.

Chapter Three

1. "Not Even Good Pornography," *Reporter,* October 20, 1955, p. 46.

2. Not so strange, perhaps, if one thinks of the example of D. H. Lawrence. For Mailer's hatred of pornography, see especially *The Presidential Papers,* p. 12, and *Advertisements for Myself,* p. 181.

3. *American Social Fiction* (New York: Barnes & Noble, 1964), pp. 162–63.

4. *Writers at Work:* The Paris Review *Interviews,* Third Series, p. 269.

5. See, for example, Podhoretz, p. 387; Donald L. Kaufmann, *Norman Mailer: The Countdown* (Carbondale and Edwardsville: Southern Illinois University Press, 1969), pp. 23–34; Helen Weinberg, *The New Novel in America* (Ithaca: Cornell University Press, 1970), pp. 112–24.

6. "Novelist Going Places," *Commentary,* 20 (December 1955), 582.

7. *The Deer Park* (New York: G. P. Putnam's Sons, 1955). Unless otherwise noted, all page references in this chapter are to this edition.

8. See Max F. Schulz, *Radical Sophistication* (Athens: Ohio University Press, 1969), pp. 81–90.

9. This point is anticipated by Podhoretz, pp. 385–86.

10. *Ibid.,* p. 385.

11. Like Munshin, Sammy was once an office boy and more than a little

"shameless." Moreover, his dealings with Julian Blumberg are such that Munshin might have come upon his "writing" methods in the pages of Budd Schulberg's *What Makes Sammy Run?* (New York: Random House, 1941).

12. Weinberg, p. 120.

13. Cf. Mailer's remark to James Baldwin: "I want to know how power works . . . how it really works in detail" (James Baldwin, "The Black Boy Looks at the White Boy," *Esquire*, 55 [May 1961], 105).

14. *Writers at Work: The Paris Review Interviews*, Third Series, p. 270.

15. *Norman Mailer*, p. 39.

16. *Writers at Work: The Paris Review Interviews*, Third Series, p. 270.

17. Mailer plays on this resemblance in his dramatized version of *The Deer Park*. After Eitel has outlined his script, Munshin remarks, "Parenthetically, I can say this is a snitch from *Miss Lonelyhearts.*" To which Eitel replies, "It was an influence." See *The Deer Park: A Play* (New York: Dial Press, 1967), p. 112.

18. *Down Mailer's Way*, p. 56.

19. See "Introduction," *A Farewell to Arms* (New York: Charles Scribner's Sons, 1948), p. viii.

Chapter Four

1. This view is held by almost every critic who has written on the novel, including Mailer himself (see *Adv*, 94). For this reason, and because the novel's formal problem is roughly the same as that in Mailer's later and more interesting experiments, *An American Dream* and *Why Are We in Vietnam?*, I have decided against any detailed discussion of the book.

2. See Sheldon Sacks, *Fiction and the Shape of Belief* (Berkeley and Los Angeles: University of California Press, 1964), especially chapters one and five.

3. Granville Hicks, "A Literary Hoax?" *Saturday Review*, March 20, 1965, p. 24; Philip Rahv, "Crime Without Punishment," *New York Review of Books*, March 25, 1965, p. 4; Elizabeth Hardwick, "Bad Boy," *Partisan Review*, 32 (Spring 1965), 291.

4. See, for example, Tom Wolfe, "Son of Crime and Punishment; Or, How to Go Eight Fast Rounds with the Heavyweight Champ—and Lose," *Book Week*, March 14, 1965, pp. 1, 10, 12–13; Joseph Epstein, "Norman X: The Literary Man's Cassius Clay," *New Republic*, April 17, 1965, pp. 22–25; Hyman, pp. 16–17.

5. *An American Dream* (New York: Dial Press, 1965). Page references to this work are incorporated into the text.

6. "Mr. Mailer Interviews Himself," *New York Times Book Review*, September 17, 1967, p. 40.

7. See John William Corrington, "An American Dreamer," *Chicago Review*, 18 (1965), 61; Kaufmann, p. 41; Adams, *Existential Battles: The Growth of Norman Mailer*, p. 78; Jean Radford, *Norman Mailer: A Critical*

Study (New York: Harper & Row, 1975), p. 101; Stanley T. Gutman, *Mankind in Barbary: The Individual and Society in the Novels of Norman Mailer* (Hanover: University Press of New England, 1975), p. 95.

8. See John W. Aldridge, "The New Energy of Success," in *Norman Mailer: A Collection of Critical Essays,* ed. Leo Braudy (Englewood Cliffs: Prentice-Hall, 1972), p. 118.

9. See Leo Bersani, "The Interpretation of Dreams," *Partisan Review,* 32 (Fall 1965), 603–608, and Nathan A. Scott, Jr., *Three American Moralists: Mailer, Bellow, and Trilling* (Notre Dame; Notre Dame University Press, 1973), pp. 56–70.

10. "The Interpretation of Dreams," p. 603.

11. Vincent Canby, "When Irish Eyes Are Smiling, It's Norman Mailer," *New York Times,* October 27, 1968, p. 15.

12. Quoted in Kaufmann, pp. 44, 45.

13. *Down Mailer's Way,* p. 137.

14. "A Short Public Notice," *Partisan Review,* 32 (Spring 1965), 181.

15. John W. Aldridge, "The Big Comeback of Norman Mailer," *Life,* March 19, 1965, p. 12.

16. See *The Presidential Papers,* p. 26; *The Armies of the Night,* pp. 38, 87; *Existential Errands,* p. 104.

17. *Down Mailer's Way,* p. 133.

18. *Fiction and the Shape of Belief,* p. 26.

19. "Crime Without Punishment," p. 4.

20. Quoted in Kaufmann, p. 44.

21. See *Down Mailer's Way,* pp. 124-77.

22. See Adams, "Existential Aesthetics: An Interview with Norman Mailer," p. 198.

23. *Mankind in Barbary: The Individual and Society in the Novels of Norman Mailer,* p. 100.

24. *Down Mailer's Way,* p. 171.

25. See *The Presidential Papers,* pp. 151, 160, 192, 213–15, 245–47, 295, and *Cannibals and Christians,* pp. 312–75, especially pp. 325, 363.

26. "A Fear of Dying: Norman Mailer's *An American Dream,*" *Hollins Critic,* 2 (June 1965), 1–11.

27. See Adams, "Existential Aesthetics: An Interview with Norman Mailer," pp. 199–201.

28. *Down Mailer's Way,* p. 173. Solotaroff's discussion anticipates my own in a number of ways, but he tends to concentrate more specifically on the mixture of realistic and unrealistic techniques in *An American Dream.* Also, he does not extend his reservations to *Why Are We in Vietnam?.*

29. *Why Are We in Vietnam?* (New York: G. P. Putnam's Sons, 1967). Page references to this edition will be incorporated into the text.

30. *Norman Mailer,* p. 129.

31. "Mr. Mailer Interviews Himself," p. 40.

32. *The Armies of the Night,* p. 188.

33. See especially Richard Pearce, "Norman Mailer's *Why Are We in Vietnam?*: A Radical Critique of Frontier Values," *Modern Fiction Studies,* 17 (Autumn 1971), 413, and Rubin Rabinovitz, "Myth and Animism in *Why Are We in Vietnam?*," *Twentieth Century Literature,* 20 (October 1974), 303.

34. See Solotaroff, p. 199; Gutman, pp. 137–38; Radford, p. 38; Richard D. Finholt, " 'Otherwise How Explain?': Norman Mailer's New Cosmology," *Modern Fiction Studies,* 17 (Autumn 1971), 378–79.

35. As D. J. elegantly puts it, "You never know what vision has been humping you through the night" (p. 208).

36. "Mailer's New Style," *Novel,* 2 (Fall 1968), 77. See also Roger Ramsey, "Current and Recurrent: The Vietnam Novel," *Modern Fiction Studies,* 17 (Autumn 1971), 427.

37. *Norman Mailer,* p. 149.

38. *The Fabulators* (New York: Oxford University Press, 1967), pp. 12, 11.

39. *Norman Mailer,* p. 120.

40. *Counter-Statement* (Los Altos: Hermes Publications, 1953), p. 124.

Chapter Five

1. Foster, p. 41.

2. *Of a Fire on the Moon* (Boston: Little, Brown and Company, 1970), p. 7.

3. *Miami and the Siege of Chicago* (New York: New American Library, 1968), p. 56.

4. Mailer's distaste for statistics is most obvious in his foreword to *The Idol and the Octopus* (New York: Dell, 1968). Here he recommends the "position papers" in his collection as "superior to the position papers of nearly all candidates" *because* they offer no statistics (p. 11).

5. "Reflections in a Bloodshot Eye," *New Statesman,* September 20, 1968, p. 351.

6. I reserve any reference to *Existential Errands,* Mailer's latest miscellany, until chapter seven, where I will consider his more recent nonfiction.

7. *The Structured Vision of Norman Mailer,* p. 224.

8. *Norman Mailer: The Countdown,* p. 151.

9. Rolo, p. 168; "What Might Have Been," p. 127; "The Crack-Up," *Time,* November 2, 1959, p. 90.

10. Laura Adams presents a similar argument but draws very different conclusions (*Existential Battles: The Growth of Norman Mailer,* pp. 27–64).

11. Phoebe Adams, review of *The Presidential Papers, Atlantic Monthly,* 212 (December 1963), 168.

12. "Why Mailer Wants to be President," *New Republic,* February 8, 1964, p. 24.

13. Mailer's earlier "poems" are collected in *Deaths for the Ladies (and other disasters).* None of Mailer's books is less deserving of serious analysis.

14. *The Armies of the Night,* pp. 124, 180, 185.

15. I have reluctantly decided against treating Mailer's literary pieces in this chapter. I do this for reasons of space, but also because I discuss Mailer's literary criticism in chapters four and seven.

16. *The Idol and the Octopus*, p. 12.

17. *The Crack-Up*, ed. Edmund Wilson (New York: New Directions, 1956), p. 75.

Chapter Six

1. See Brower, p. 100.

2. *The Armies of the Night* (New York: New American Library, 1968). Unless otherwise noted, all page references in this chapter are to this edition.

3. *Of a Fire on the Moon*, p. 141.

4. Book one of *Armies* was first published in *Harper's*, March 1968. Book two was later published in *Commentary*, April 1968.

5. For a good discussion of how Hemingway structured his book along these lines, see Carlos Baker, *Hemingway: The Writer as Artist*, 3rd. ed. rev. (Princeton: Princeton University Press, 1963), pp. 169–71.

6. George Plimpton, "The Story Behind a Nonfiction Novel," *New York Times Book Review*, January 16, 1966, p. 41.

7. *Ibid.*

8. David Galloway, "Why the Chickens Came Home to Roost in Holcomb, Kansas: Truman Capote's *In Cold Blood*," in *Truman Capote's* In Cold Blood: *A Critical Handbook*, ed. Irving Malin (Belmont: Wadsworth Publishing Company, 1968), pp. 155–56.

9. Miller is almost certainly more "accurate" than Capote, for the simple reason that he usually writes about what he has experienced firsthand, while Capote must often rely on witnesses who don't agree on points major and minor. For a revealing discussion of Capote's dilemma in choosing among conflicting sources, see Phillip K. Tompkins, "In Cold Fact," *Esquire*, 65 (June 1966), 125, 127, 166–71.

10. Tompkins has shown that Capote, in his portrait of Perry Smith, includes episodes and details which are at best very unreliable. See *ibid.*, pp. 127, 166–71.

11. "Death in Kansas," *Spectator*, March 18, 1966, p. 331.

12. See *The Armies of the Night*, pp. 59–60, 120–21, 260–62, 272–76. Mailer also cites sources in order to refute them. See pp. 3–4, 214–15.

13. Capote has described these pieces as just such a training ground for *In Cold Blood*. See Plimpton, p. 2.

14. *The Electric Kool-Aid Acid Test* (New York: Bantam Books, 1969), p. 371.

15. This distinction is a bit crude, for of course certain fictions are shaped by rhetorical ends. Nonetheless, most novels are not so structured. My argument here again relies on Sacks' *Fiction and the Shape of Belief*, especially chapter one.

16. But see Solotaroff's intelligent comparison of the two works, pp. 219–22, and also Gordon O. Taylor's discussion of the two writers, "Of Adams and Aquarius," *American Literature*, 46 (March 1974), 68–82.

17. "Introduction," *The Education of Henry Adams* (Boston: Houghton Mifflin, 1961), p. v.

18. See Charles Reich, *The Greening of America* (New York: Random House, 1970), and John W. Aldridge, *In the Country of the Young* (New York: Harper's Magazine Press, 1970).

Chapter Seven

1. *The Faith of Graffiti* (New York: Praeger, 1974). Other works of this period will be cited in the text as follows: *Miami and the Siege of Chicago* as *MC*; *Of a Fire on the Moon* as *Fire*; *The Prisoner of Sex* as *PS*; *Existential Errands* as *EE*; *Marilyn: A Biography* (New York: Grosset & Dunlap, 1973) as *M*; *Genius and Lust: A Journey Through the Major Writings of Henry Miller* (New York: Grove Press, 1976) as *GL*.

2. For Mailer's resistance to the label of "journalist," see *The Armies of the Night*, p. 22, and *Of a Fire on the Moon*, p. 7. For his more recent acceptance of the title, see *Existential Errands*, p. ix.

3. "Norman Mailer: The Embattled Vision," p. 371.

4. *The Armies of the Night*, p. 22.

5. *Down Mailer's Way*, p. 238.

6. Warner Berthoff, "Witness and Testament: Two Contemporary Classics," in *Aspects of Narrative*, ed. J. Hillis Miller (New York: Columbia University Press, 1971), p. 196.

7. "The Aesthetics of Norman Mailer," in *Norman Mailer: The Man and His Work*, ed. Robert F. Lucid (Boston: Little, Brown and Company, 1971), p. 199.

8. For examples of this oft repeated claim, see *Advertisements for Myself*, p. 93, and *The Armies of the Night*, p. 25.

9. See "The Ups and Downs of Mailer," *New Republic*, January 23, 1971, pp. 23–26.

10. I don't mean to imply that Mailer was to abandon entirely the reporting of historical events. *St. George and the Godfather* (New York: New American Library, 1972) and *The Fight* (Boston: Little, Brown and Company, 1975), undistinguished as they are, testify to Mailer's continuing attraction to this kind of reportage even as he was seeking other outlets for his method.

11. "Meditations on Norman Mailer, by Norman Mailer, Against the Day a Norman Mailest Comes Along," *New York Times Book Review*, May 23, 1971, p. 1.

12. For Kate Millett's discussion of these writers, see *Sexual Politics* (New York: Equinox Books, 1971), pp. 237–361.

13. *Norman Mailer: A Critical Study*, pp. 155–59.

14. *Ibid.*, p. 157.

15. As Laura Adams points out, Zolotow's complaint was that Mailer had quoted more passages than his publishers paid for, not that Mailer had "stolen" his work. Adams also remarks that Zolotow eventually apologized for the accusation (*Existential Battles: The Growth of Norman Mailer*, p. 181n).

16. Ingrid Bengis, "Monroe According to Mailer: One Legend Feeds on Another," *MS.*, 11 (October 1973), 47.

17. Mailer's first comments on Miller appeared in *Cannibals and Christians*, p. 198. More recently he has published extended discussions of Miller in *The Prisoner of Sex*, pp. 73–92, and *American Review 24*, ed. Theodore Solotaroff (New York, 1976), pp. 1–40. Both discussions are incorporated into Mailer's *Genius and Lust* commentary.

Chapter Eight

1. "Norman Mailer: The Pride of Vulnerability," *Norman Mailer: A Collection of Critical Essays*, p. 1.

2. *Existential Battles: The Growth of Norman Mailer*, p. 9.

Selected Bibliography

PRIMARY SOURCES

1. Fiction:

An American Dream. New York: Dial Press, 1965.
Barbary Shore. New York: Holt, Rinehart and Winston, 1951.
The Deer Park. New York: G. P. Putnam's Sons, 1955.
The Naked and the Dead. New York: Holt, Rinehart and Winston, 1948.
The Short Fiction of Norman Mailer. New York: Dell, 1967.
Why Are We in Vietnam? New York: G. P. Putnam's Sons, 1967.

2. Nonfiction:

The Armies of the Night: History as a Novel / The Novel as History. New York: New American Library, 1968.
The Faith of Graffiti. New York: Praeger, 1974.
The Fight. Boston: Little, Brown and Company, 1975.
Genius and Lust: A Journey Through the Major Writings of Henry Miller. New York: Grove Press, 1976.
King of the Hill. New York: New American Library, 1971.
Marilyn: A Biography. New York: Grosset & Dunlap, 1973.
Miami and the Siege of Chicago. New York: New American Library, 1968.
Of a Fire on the Moon. Boston: Little, Brown and Company, 1970.
The Prisoner of Sex. Boston: Little, Brown and Company, 1971.
Some Honorable Men: Political Conventions, 1960–1972. Boston: Little, Brown and Company, 1976.
St. George and the Godfather. New York: New American Library, 1972 (on the 1972 political conventions).
The White Negro: Superficial Reflections on the Hipster. San Francisco: City Lights Books, 1957.

3. Miscellanies:

Advertisements for Myself. New York: G. P. Putnam's Sons, 1959.
Cannibals and Christians. New York: Dial Press, 1966.
Existential Errands. Boston: Little, Brown and Company, 1972.
The Presidential Papers. New York: G. P. Putnam's Sons, 1963.

4. Miscellaneous Writings:

The Bullfight: A Photographic Narrative with Text by Norman Mailer. New York: CBS Legacy Collection Book, distributed by MacMillan, 1967 (accompanied by a long-playing record of poetry of Federico Garcia Lorca and of Norman Mailer reading from his "Footnote to *Death in the Afternoon,*" with background music and "authentic location recordings").

Deaths for the Ladies (and other disasters). New York: G. P. Putnam's Sons, 1962 (poems).

The Deer Park: A Play. New York: Dial Press, 1967.

The Idol and the Octopus: Political Writings by Norman Mailer on the Kennedy and Johnson Administrations. New York: New American Library, 1968.

Maidstone: A Mystery. New York: New American Library, 1971 (film script).

SECONDARY SOURCES

The literature on Mailer is extensive, so I have had to be quite selective. I have included all books published on Mailer and those essays which I think most useful for the study of his works. The most complete bibliography (through the early 1970s) is Laura Adams' *Norman Mailer: A Comprehensive Bibliography* (Metuchen, New Jersey: Scarecrow Press, 1974).

1. Books

ADAMS, LAURA. *Existential Battles: The Growth of Norman Mailer.* Athens: Ohio University Press, 1976. Concerned with the evolution of Mailer's thought in relation to his art. Adds little to Solotaroff's earlier study of the subject.

FLAHERTY, JOE. *Managing Mailer.* New York: Coward-McCann, 1969. An amusing account of Mailer's mayoralty race in 1969.

FOSTER, RICHARD. *Norman Mailer.* Minneapolis: University of Minnesota Press, 1968. This pamphlet is probably the best short introduction to Mailer's career through 1967.

GUTMAN, STANLEY T. *Mankind in Barbary: The Individual and Society in the Novels of Norman Mailer.* Hanover, New Hampshire: University Press of New England, 1975. Another attempt to explain Mailer's thematic development which merely confirms Solotaroff's insights.

KAUFMANN, DONALD L. *Norman Mailer: The Countdown.* Carbondale and Edwardsville: Southern Illinois University Press, 1969. The most uneven full-length study of Mailer. Very weak on the novels but pioneering on Mailer's social and political ideas.

LEEDS, BARRY H. *The Structured Vision of Norman Mailer.* New York: New York University Press, 1969. Develops the unconvincing thesis that

Mailer's canon reveals a consistent evolution from "pessimistic" to "positive" themes.

MIDDLEBROOK, JONATHAN. *Mailer and the Times of His Time*. San Francisco: Bay Books, 1976. An unpersuasive defense of the notion that Mailer is a latter-day Transcendentalist.

Norman Mailer: A Collection of Critical Essays. Ed. Leo Braudy. Englewood Cliffs, New Jersey: Prentice-Hall, 1972. The best collection of essays on Mailer. Includes two excellent essays published here for the first time, Michael Cowan's "The Americanness of Norman Mailer" and editor Leo Braudy's "Norman Mailer: The Pride of Vulnerability."

Norman Mailer: The Man and His Work. Ed. Robert F. Lucid. Boston: Little, Brown and Company, 1971. A useful collection of essays and reviews on Mailer first published in the 1960s.

POIRIER, RICHARD. *Norman Mailer*. New York: Viking Press, 1972. A difficult study which argues that Mailer's virtues are those of a stylist and "performer," not those of a literary craftsman. Everywhere intelligent but tied to its dubious thesis.

RADFORD, JEAN. *Norman Mailer: A Critical Study*. New York: Harper & Row, 1975. Yet another study of Mailer's intellectual development. Intelligent but insufficiently original.

SOLOTAROFF, ROBERT. *Down Mailer's Way*. Urbana: University of Illinois Press, 1974. The most thorough treatment of Mailer's intellectual growth. The best book on Mailer and one of the better books on any contemporary American writer.

WEATHERBY, W. J. *Squaring Off: Mailer vs. Baldwin*. New York: Mason/Charter, 1977. An account of Mailer's personal and literary relations with James Baldwin. Interesting for its biographical, not its literary, implications.

Will the Real Norman Mailer Please Stand Up? Ed. Laura Adams. Port Washington, New York: Kennikat Press, 1974. The latest collection of critical essays on Mailer. Includes several previously unpublished assessments.

2. Book Excerpts and Articles

BERTHOFF, WARNER. "Witness and Testament: Two Contemporary Classics," *Aspects of Narrative*, Ed. J. Hillis Miller, New York: Columbia University Press, 1971, pp. 173–98. The second half of this essay offers the best published discussion of *The Armies of the Night*.

DICKSTEIN, MORRIS. *Gates of Eden: American Culture in the Sixties*. New York: Basic Books, 1977. Includes several discussions of Mailer's works. Especially good on the nonfiction.

FOSTER, RICHARD. "Mailer and the Fitzgerald Tradition." *Novel*, 1 (Spring 1968), 219–30. Like Michael Cowan's essay (see *Norman Mailer: A Collection of Critical Essays*, under "Books" above), an impressive attempt to define the nature of Mailer's romanticism.

KAUFMANN, DONALD L. "The Long Happy Life of Norman Mailer." *Modern Fiction Studies*, 17 (Autumn 1971), 347–59. A first-rate discussion of Mailer and Hemingway which emphasizes the differences between these often associated writers.

LANGBAUM, ROBERT. "Mailer's New Style." *Novel*, 2 (Fall 1968), 69–78. One of the first and more impressive attempts to argue that *An American Dream* and *Why Are We in Vietnam?* represent a viable new "style" for Mailer's fiction.

LUCID, ROBERT F. "Three Public Performances: Fitzgerald, Hemingway, Mailer." *American Scholar*, 43 (Summer 1974), 447–66. An extremely well written essay which examines in part the nature of Mailer's public "legend."

MERRILL, ROBERT. *"The Armies of the Night:* The Education of Norman Mailer." *Illinois Quarterly*, 37 (September 1974), 30–44. A formal analysis stressing the ways in which Books One and Two are related.

———. "Norman Mailer's Early Nonfiction: The Art of Self-Revelation." *Western Humanities Review*, 28 (Winter 1974), 1–12. A study of Mailer's emerging persona in the essays preceding *The Armies of the Night*.

MILLER, JAMES E., JR. "The Creation of Women: Confessions of a Shaken Liberal." *Centennial Review*, 18 (Summer 1974), 231–47. Includes an unsympathetic discussion of Mailer's quarrel with Kate Millett.

MUSTE, JOHN M. "Norman Mailer and John Dos Passos: The Question of Influence." *Modern Fiction Studies*, 17 (Autumn 1971), 361–74. A perceptive analysis of *The Naked and the Dead* which radically qualifies the common view that Dos Passos was a major influence on Mailer's book.

PODHORETZ, NORMAN. "Norman Mailer: The Embattled Vision." *Partisan Review*, 26 (Summer 1959), 371–91. The first general essay on Mailer and still one of the better ones.

SCHRADER, GEORGE A. "Norman Mailer and the Despair of Defiance." *Yale Review*, 51 (December 1961), 267–80. A rigorous, incisive attack on the philosophical assumptions of Mailer's hipsterism.

TANNER, TONY. "On the Parapet (Norman Mailer)," *City of Words: American Fiction 1950–1970*, New York: Harper & Row, 1971, pp. 344–71. The best single essay on Mailer's novels, devoted mainly to their evolving themes.

TAYLOR, GORDON O. "Of Adams and Aquarius." *American Literature*, 46 (March 1974), 68–82. A fine study of *The Education of Henry Adams* and *Of a Fire on the Moon* which traces remarkable parallels between the two books.

TRILLING, DIANA. "The Radical Moralism of Norman Mailer," *Claremont Essays*, New York: Harcourt Brace Jovanovich, 1962, pp. 175–202. Like Podhoretz's essay, an early study of enduring value. Focuses on Mailer's passionate commitment to ideas.

WALDRON, RANDALL H. "The Naked, the Dead, and the Machine: A New Look at Norman Mailer's First Novel." *PMLA*, 87 (March 1972), 271–77. An interesting reassessment of *The Naked and the Dead*, marred by its insistence that Mailer's intentions were those of a conventional liberal.

Index

Names of characters in Mailer's novels are followed by the title, in parentheses, of the work in which they appear.

166